Mission Possible!

*Cycle B Sermons
for Advent, Christmas, and Epiphany
Based on the Gospel Texts*

Charley Reeb

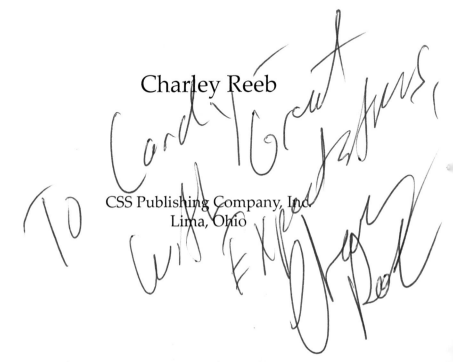

CSS Publishing Company, Inc.
Lima, Ohio

MISSION POSSIBLE!

FIRST EDITION
Copyright © 2014
by CSS Publishing Co., Inc.

Library of Congress Cataloging-in-Publication Data

Reeb, Charles D., 1973-
Mission possible! : Cycle B sermons for Advent, Christmas, and Epiphany based on the gospel texts / Charley Reeb.
pages cm
ISBN 0-7880-2787-5 (alk. paper)
1. Bible. Gospels--Sermons. 2. Sermons, American--21st century. 3. Advent sermons. 4. Christmas sermons. 5. Epiphany season--Sermons. 6. Church year sermons. 7. Common lectionary (1992). Year B. I. Title.

BS2555.54.R44 2014
252'.61--dc23

2014014831

For more information about CSS Publishing Company resources, visit our website at www.csspub.com, email us at csr@csspub.com, or call (800) 241-4056.

e-book
ISBN-13: 978-0-7880-2788-8
ISBN-10: 0-7880-2788-3

ISBN-13: 978-0-7880-2787-1
ISBN-10: 0-7880-2787-5   PRINTED IN USA

To J.D. — an answer to prayer

Foreword

This book was written to help those who are looking for ways to enhance their spiritual journeys during the seasons of Advent, Christmas, and Epiphany. These messages are based on the Revised Common Lectionary, which are the assigned scripture passages for each Sunday of the church year. Some may choose to read this book for personal study and reflection as they follow the lectionary on their own. Others may wish to use it in their local churches. Those churches that follow the lectionary could utilize this book as curriculum for Sunday school classes, Bible studies, and other small groups. Small group leaders may wish to prepare questions based on these messages and use those questions to facilitate discussions.

This book was also written for preachers who are looking for ideas and illustrations for sermons. One of the most demanding tasks for a preacher is to prepare fresh, dynamic, and inspiring sermons week after week for the same congregation. This is especially true in the season of Advent when seeking to interpret the same story yet again in new and exciting ways. The hope is that these messages will provide insights and stories that will aid preachers in the preparation of sermons. The messages in this book were preached to a local congregation and have been "road tested."

An effective way for preachers to use this book would be to develop their own table of contents to refer back to when an insight or illustration is needed. When something useful is found, highlight it and then write in the front of the book or on a separate piece of paper a summary sentence about the topic highlighted along with the page number. This will save a great deal of time when Sunday is quickly approaching and fresh content is needed.

However you choose to use this book my prayer is that you will be encouraged by one common theme weaved throughout these messages — we can have hope because God makes the impossible possible. From a virgin conceiving a child to that child growing up and transforming people as well as the world, these messages point to God's revelation to us in Christ. This revelation pierces our darkness, brings hope to a hopeless world, and empowers us, by the grace of God, to see and do what seems impossible.

I want to thank Pasadena Community Church for their loving support and encouragement as I prepared and preached these messages. It is a true joy to serve this congregation. I am also grateful for my wife Brandy. Her love and unwavering support provide strength for a calling that is always challenging yet equally rewarding.

Table of Contents

Advent 1
Mark 13:24-37

But in those days, after that suffering, the sun will be darkened, and the moon will not give its light, and the stars will be falling from heaven, and the powers in the heavens will be shaken. Then they will see "the Son of Man coming in clouds" with great power and glory. Then he will send out the angels, and gather his elect from the four winds, from the ends of the earth to the ends of heaven. From the fig tree learn its lesson: as soon as its branch becomes tender and puts forth its leaves, you know that summer is near. So also, when you see these things taking place, you know that he is near, at the very gates. Truly I tell you, this generation will not pass away until all these things have taken place. Heaven and earth will pass away, but my words will not pass away. But about that day or hour no one knows, neither the angels in heaven, nor the Son, but only the Father. Beware, keep alert; for you do not know when the time will come. It is like a man going on a journey, when he leaves home and puts his slaves in charge, each with his work, and commands the doorkeeper to be on the watch. Therefore, keep awake — for you do not know when the master of the house will come, in the evening, or at midnight, or at cockcrow, or at dawn, or else he may find you asleep when he comes suddenly. And what I say to you I say to all: Keep awake.

Three Things
You Can Count On

One summer I took a month off for a much needed time of renewal. During my time off I decided to do a little research. I wanted to get the perspective of folks who don't go to church. Preachers are very insulated in a church bubble. Everything we do revolves around church culture for the most part and that is not all bad. But here is the thing — if the church's main task is to reach those outside of it then it would be wise for me to get the pulse of those outside the church bubble. How can we be effective at reaching others with the gospel if we don't seek to understand what they do, where they live, how they hurt, and what their hang-ups are about religion?

One of the things I decided to do during my time away was not to tell the people I met that I was a preacher. All kinds of baggage and transference surfaces when you do that. I wanted an honest perspective. For example, one Sunday morning I didn't go to worship. Instead, I went to that great American institution, the "Waffle House"! I got to know our waitress. I found out she had two kids and was working two jobs to make ends meet. Some of the hardest working people in America are waitresses at the "Waffle House." She told me how long she had been working there and explained what "scattered, smothered, and covered" meant. Then she told me that around 11 a.m. on Sundays they start to get real busy because that is when the church crowd comes in. I thought, "Here is my chance!" I asked, "What are the church people like?" She replied, "Most of them are terrible tippers." I don't know if she goes to church, but her impression of a church crowd is that they are not very generous. So I filed that away — "Impression of church folk: lack generosity."

Another time I sat at a bar and grill out of town for lunch and struck up a conversation with the bartender. I sat there with my Coke and asked a few benign questions. I found out that she grew up in bars her whole life. Her parents owned a bar. When she wasn't working at a bar she went to bars and hung out with people. I said, "I'm curious. You have a unique perspective being around bars all of your life. What's the most important thing you have learned?" She replied, "Never trust anybody who says, 'You can trust me.' " Then she said, "And I have learned that the only person you can count on is yourself." I filed that one away — "Trust is a very important issue."

Perhaps the most striking conversation I had was on a golf course when I was out of town. I was by myself and was paired up with a couple of people. I made sure they didn't find out I was a preacher. When most golfers find out you're a preacher they stop being fun! They also expect you to give them three foot putts! I got to know a guy in the group who was in sales. He had taken a big hit in the recession and was trying to get his feet back on the ground. He had just gone through a bitter divorce and was going through other personal struggles. He said, "The older I get the less I find things to believe in." Then he railed against politics, religion, and anything else he could think of. At the end of the round he asked, "What can you really believe in?"

That question echoed in my mind for days. If I was to run into that guy again, what would I say? What would you say? That really is the feeling of so many people in our culture today. What can you really believe in? What can you really count on in life? In fact, most of the conversations I had with strangers during my time off reflected cynicism about life. Those conversations reminded me of the words of

Ecclesiastes, " 'Vanity of vanities,' says the teacher, 'vanity of vanities, all is vanity… for all is vanity and chasing after the wind' " (Ecclesiastes 1:2; 2:11). You can translate the word "vanity" as "emptiness" or "meaningless." The writer of Ecclesiastes came to the conclusion that all of life is empty. Self-indulgence and even hard work leads to emptiness.

It is easy to be cynical in our world and come to this conclusion. It is easy to feel like that man on the golf course, "The older I get the less I find things to believe in. What can you really believe in?" It is easy to feel like the bartender who said, "Never trust anyone who says, 'You can trust me.' " It all feels so empty. Nothing is new. Nothing satisfies. You may be hitting mid-life and feel that way. All the goals and ambitions you set for yourself have lost their luster. Nothing seems new and exciting anymore and you feel stuck. You may be a tired, worn out parent who feels that every day is the same — same routine with the kids, same car pool, same schedule, no change, nothing new. You may be retired and feel you have lost the meaning in your life you once had. You feel it has slipped away. Will you be remembered? Will everything you have done be forgotten? Is it all empty? Is it all chasing after the wind?

I have thought a lot about that question — "What can you really believe in?" If someone asked that again, what would I say? How would you answer that question?

As we begin the Advent season we focus on the things we can believe in. This season is all about preparing ourselves to receive the light of Christ that pierces our dark and cynical world. A good place to start is Jesus' words in our assigned lesson in Mark, "Heaven and earth will pass away, but my words will not pass away" (Mark 13:31). This is a comforting and encouraging truth. The world may crumble to the ground but Jesus and his words will last forever. The revelation of God in Jesus Christ provides the ultimate stability in an unstable world.

There are three ways we can break down the eternal truth of God's revelation to us in Christ. These are three things we can believe in when the world is falling apart. These three things will be true for eternity. The first thing: God is.

After twenty years of preaching and about twelve years of academic theological study, I have learned two irrefutable facts — there is a God and I am not him! There is a God and none of us are him! That seems to be a rather simple thing to understand but it is amazing how many people forget it. In fact, what troubles me the most about Christians today is how many feel they have a monopoly on God. When you talk to some Christians they think God can be summed up in a theological formula or a spiritual law. It's like they have God in their back pocket. They may not think they are God but they think they have God all figured out and if you don't think of God on their terms with their language and their systems then you are on the outside. The theological arrogance within the Christian landscape today is staggering.

God is bigger, wider, deeper, and longer than our finite minds can fathom. God cannot be contained by our language and formulas. If God were small enough for us to contain he wouldn't be worth believing in! God is mystery and uncontainable. God is bigger than our theological systems. God is bigger than our political ideas. God is bigger than denominations. God is bigger than the church. God is bigger than the Bible. Now, these things are important and they have their place but they cannot contain God. Nothing can! All of our language of God is a limited metaphor for his power, glory, love, and grace.

The older I get and the more I grow as a Christian the bigger God gets and the more open I am to discovering the depth of who God is. I submit to you that all Christian growth goes in that direction. The moment we think we have God figured out, we don't! God says through Isaiah, "My ways are higher than your ways, my thoughts are greater than your thoughts" (Isaiah 55:9). And there is great comfort, security, and trust that come from this — that the God who created this world has got it in his hands. And this God doesn't think like you or I do. He doesn't respond the way we would respond. God's ways are higher than our ways. I take great comfort from that.

There are certain non-negotiables about God. We call that dogma — God is love; God is creator, redeemer, sustainer, and more. But after dogma you have doctrine and opinion and these are flexible and up for debate. There is a relatively small amount of dogma about God and a large amount of doctrine and opinion about God. The sad thing is that much of the history of the Christian church is about the disunity that has occurred through the years over doctrine and opinion.

How can we really know and understand this great big God if he is bigger than we can fathom? This leads me to the second thing we can believe in: God can be known and experienced in Jesus Christ.

Colossians says that Christ is "the image of the invisible God" (Colossians 1:15). We may disagree on the interpretation of scripture. We may disagree politically. We may disagree on the stance Christians take on particular issues. We may disagree on doctrine and theology. But one thing we as Christians can stand together on is that God's love and grace can be known and experienced in and through Jesus Christ. You want to know what God is like? Read the gospels and see God in flesh and blood reaching out to the world and saving it.

My wife Brandy and I have a dog named PJ. She is a Jack Russell and she is completely blind. She can't see us at all but she knows us and trusts us because of the way we encounter her and help her. When we guide her on walks she knows we love her and she can trust us. When we pick her up and put her on the bed she knows we love her and she can trust us.

One day Brandy took PJ out to use the bathroom. Up to this point we didn't use a leash because she stayed contained in a particular area. But on this particular day she sensed a bird and blindly ran after it. She ended up jumping over the sea wall! I heard Brandy scream and I ran out. I saw Brandy climbing over the sea wall and rescuing PJ. PJ's tongue was hanging out of her mouth and her tail was just wagging.

You know, it is the same with us. We are blind. We cannot know God on our own. We can't save ourselves. Left to our own devices we are lost. So Christ encounters us, picks us up, and rescues us from sin and death. He rescues us from ourselves and puts us on the right path. We can't see God but in Christ we know he is love and that love is all that matters.

At the end of the day, what matters is not which church we belong to, what theological doctrine we hold, or what theological system we believe in. What matters is knowing and experiencing God's love in Jesus Christ. That's what matters. All else is secondary. Why? Here is the third thing we can believe in: The experience of God's love in Christ transforms people.

Doctrine doesn't change people. Theological systems don't change people. Denominations and institutions don't change people. God's love and grace experienced in Christ changes people. I've seen people walk down the aisle and receive healing from the forgiveness of their sins. I've seen marriages and lives saved, relationships restored, and great healing come all because of the love of God experienced in Christ. That's what the church is about — being a vessel for people to be transformed by God's love in Christ.

A colleague once shared a story about a woman in his church who experienced transformation. At 45 years old she was a wreck. She was divorced with kids and had no job or motivation. She visited his church and heard about Jesus and his love. One Sunday morning she received Christ as her Lord and Savior. The experience completely awakened her. She went to college and paid her way through an administrative assistant job. She got a B.A. cum laude and a Masters degree with all A's in her field. She wrote him an email that spoke of her experience: "Isn't Jesus amazing? I don't know why more Christians don't believe in the miracles of Jesus. I believe in them. He healed me. What could be more miraculous than the forgiveness of sins or the taking away of all my bitterness and resentment? My peace and joy are indescribable. I laugh all the time now when I thought I would never laugh again. I am grateful beyond words... I feel like I have swallowed sunshine."

After all his complaining about the emptiness of life, the writer of Ecclesiastes came to this conclusion: "For apart from God who can eat or who can have enjoyment? For to the one who pleases him, God gives wisdom and knowledge and joy" (2:25-26).

God is. You can know and experience God in Christ. The experience of God's love in Christ transforms people. Those are three things you can believe in. You can experience that love today and be transformed. Give your heart to Christ. Amen.

Advent 2
Mark 1:1-8

The beginning of the good news of Jesus Christ, the Son of God. As it is written in the prophet Isaiah, "See, I am sending my messenger ahead of you, who will prepare your way; the voice of one crying out in the wilderness: 'Prepare the way of the Lord, make his paths straight,'" John the baptizer appeared in the wilderness, proclaiming a baptism of repentance for the forgiveness of sins. And people from the whole Judean countryside and all the people of Jerusalem were going out to him, and were baptized by him in the river Jordan, confessing their sins. Now John was clothed with camel's hair, with a leather belt around his waist, and he ate locusts and wild honey. He proclaimed, "The one who is more powerful than I is coming after me; I am not worthy to stoop down and untie the thong of his sandals. I have baptized you with water; but he will baptize you with the Holy Spirit."

While You Wait

I don't know anyone who likes to wait. Whether it is waiting in line, waiting on a package to be delivered, or waiting for a prayer to be answered, waiting is not something we usually enjoy. What we sometimes forget is that there is a great deal of wisdom in waiting. This is why Advent is so important. Advent is a good time to learn about waiting because this season is all about waiting well. For the next few weeks we sit on the edge of our seats waiting for God to come to us in Christ and transform our lives with his love. In this process of waiting for Christmas, Advent teaches us lessons about why God sometimes makes us wait.

Many of us never learn the wisdom in waiting because waiting is not always fun. That's why our culture is built around preventing this dreaded task — fast food, faster internet, faster delivery, faster service, call ahead seating, no waiting! We send a text and we love getting a text back instantly! We go on the internet and we love shopping and buying with one click. We can find a book we want and press one button and boom it is downloaded and so is our credit card! Recently the *New York Times* published an article stating that we will visit a website less often if it is slower than a close competitor by a quarter of a second. That's .25 seconds! That's way too long for any normal person to wait! We don't like to wait! We want what we want now!

The other day I was running late and when I got to the office I realized that I forgot my cell phone charger and my phone had run out of juice. I rushed frantically to see if someone had a charger I could borrow. I finally found one and I plugged it in. But here was the problem — I needed to leave the office soon with my phone and I had to have it charged at least half way for the rest of the day and I did not have a car charger. So what did I have to do? I had to wait! I just had to sit there and wait. It was so frustrating! And this was just a phone!

We don't like to wait. We think it is a waste of time. We are always rushing to the next place or the next thing. We don't like being held up.

This carries over into our spiritual lives. We want instant answers to our prayers. We want God to respond quickly to our needs. We want God to provide for us within our time frame and schedule. We have everything figured out, right? Everything makes sense to us. Why doesn't God just act? Let's get on with it, right?

Maybe you are without a job and you have been praying and praying for one and there is no response. You have interviewed, searched, and searched some more and there is nothing.

Maybe you are praying to meet the right person to develop a romantic relationship with and all you meet are duds! Or maybe you are in a relationship with someone and you have prayed and prayed for him or her to make a commitment, to show signs of wanting to marry, but there seems to be no chance of that happening.

Perhaps you need to make a really important decision about your life and you are searching for a sign, something that will tell you which way you should go, and you have come up empty. You keep looking and you can't seem to find anything from God.

Perhaps you have been praying for the ability to lose weight and get in better shape but it doesn't seem to be any easier and you can't make progress.

Maybe you are in a funk in your life — unmotivated, sad, maybe even depressed. You've asked God to give you a new spirit, more energy, and joy but you still can't seem to get off the couch.

Perhaps you are lonely, wanting to meet new people and you have been praying for God to bring new people in your life but nothing has changed.

I am sure many of you are wondering what is taking God so long to answer, to act, to move on your request! You have prayed persistently and faithfully. The Bible says, "Ask and it will be given you, seek and you shall find, knock and the door will be open to you" (Luke 11:9). You have asked until your throat is sore and you have knocked until your knuckles are bloody and yet there is still no answer! You are getting discouraged. You think, "Does God not like me? Does he not care? Is God angry with me?"

This may be hard for some of us to believe but it is because God cares for us and loves us that he often makes us wait. God always has good reasons for making us wait. Once we recognize these reasons it is easier for us to accept that waiting on God is not a waste of time. You see, this is why God is rarely in a hurry. He is usually slow in the way he operates. Regardless of how fast we want God to go, he will not go at our pace. He always has a good reason why he goes about things the way he does. We just don't see it because, well, we are not God!

So why is God so slow? Why does he so often make us wait? Discovering why God makes us wait is a game changer. It will become more important to you than anything you are waiting on God to give you right now. That may sound crazy because you feel so desperate for God to answer you but, trust me, knowing why God is making you wait will make all the difference in the world to your faith, relationships, and purpose in life.

One of the most important reasons God makes us wait is revealed through John the Baptist. John the Baptist was an interesting guy. He was the child of Mary's cousin Elizabeth.

If Rambo had been a prophet he would have been John the Baptist. John lived out in the wild. He wore camel hair and ate locusts and wild honey. But instead of carrying weapons to bring peace and justice to the world he carried words of warning and preparation. Crowds would go out into the wild and listen to him preach sermons with his hair on fire. Some would take him seriously. Others thought he was just entertaining. The truth is that God had called John to do one thing — tell people to prepare themselves for God to enter their world in the person of Christ.

The people of God had waited and waited and prayed and prayed for a Messiah to come bringing hope and healing to the world. They had longed for it. They were desperate for it. John the Baptist said that this Messiah was indeed coming and he would fulfill all the promises of their faith. But before he came John had a critical message to give to the world then and now. He gave the same sermon over and over. It was this: "Repent, for the kingdom of heaven is near" (Matthew 3:2 NIV). "Prepare the way for the Lord, make straight paths for him" (Mark 1:3 NIV).

"Repent" — that's an old-fashioned word. We think it means to feel awful about the bad things you have done. Tell God and others you are really sorry and ask for forgiveness. We may think, "Okay I get it. I just need to apologize to God and others for the bad things I have done. When I do then my prayers will be answered! I can get an apology speech ready in minutes!"

Hold on. That's not what repent means. The true biblical definition of repent means to "turn" — to turn away from the things that are not good for you and turn to God — to turn your thoughts and life to God. There's an old bumper sticker that reads, "God Allows U-Turns." That's what it means to repent. You may be thinking, "Well that's what I'm doing, isn't it? I'm praying to God and waiting for him. I'm turning to him to answer my prayer!" We will get back to that in a second.

"Prepare the way, make straight paths for him" — the image here is one of cleaning your house for an honored guest. You clean every corner and crevice, making sure everything is spotless so the Queen of England would be pleased to stay there. What John is saying is that we need to make room for Christ in our lives. We need to clear the clutter out and make our heart a place that Christ is pleased to dwell.

What does this have to do with waiting on God and getting your prayers answered? Everything! We must get our hearts and lives right with God before we should expect God to answer us. Sometimes we pray repeatedly for things and we wait until we get frustrated. But the whole time we are frustrated it is God who is waiting on us because our hearts and lives are not right with him.

It could be you have prayed that your boyfriend would propose to you but your relationship is toxic and he is not a Christian. He does not share your values and he is dragging you down, yet you are asking God to bless your marriage.

Maybe you are looking for a sign from God about whether or not to write off a friend when deep down you know you are the one who needs to ask your friend for forgiveness for something you did in the past and you have never done it.

Maybe you are disappointed God doesn't seem to be helping you get healthier when you are not making the lifestyle changes you need in order to get healthier.

It could be that you are waiting on God to snap you out of your sadness and funk when the truth is deep inside you know that this funk you are in is about the guilt you feel about a sin in your life you need to confront.

You may be praying to God for the right things but for the wrong reasons. It seems like a noble prayer to everyone else but you know it's about your ego and pride. You need to look really hard at your motives and ask, "Why am I praying for this? Is it about God or is it about me?"

I think you see where this is going. If you are someone who has been waiting for God to answer your prayer and you are desperate you might want to take a serious look at your life, your heart, your motives, and the reason behind your prayers. This may not be the reason why God is making you wait. There are other reasons why God makes us wait. All I am asking is that as you wait you think hard about where you are with God. Take a look at this life-changing passage from 1 John 5:14-15 (NIV):

> This is the confidence we have in approaching God: that if we ask anything according to his will, he hears us. And if we know that he hears us — whatever we ask — we know that we have what we asked of him.

We can have "confidence" in approaching God with our prayers knowing he will answer every one of them. But our prayers must be "according to his will." If our prayers are according to his will, we know he hears us and will answer us and we will like the answer. This assumes one big thing — that our prayers are consistent with God's interests and desires. If we find that our prayers are not, God will make us wait until they are. It is only when our lives are structured around God and his desires that our prayers will be what he desires.

The question is — this prayer you want God to answer so bad and you have been waiting for an answer to — is it really what God desires? Has it been rooted in an active relationship with him? Will it serve not only your interests but his as well?

Here is something to think about: If you think you are waiting on God, he might be waiting on *you*. God might be waiting on you to look at your heart and come back to him.

You see, God loves us too much to always give us what we want. God sees the big picture and so often what we want is not good for us nor does it serve the interests of God.

God doesn't want you to make a huge mistake that you might regret the rest of your life. He doesn't want you to go down a bad road because it is the convenient thing to do. He wants you to have life in all its abundance. He wants you to experience real life with him. He wants you to have the lasting joy that comes from being obedient to him. God always has our best interests at heart — always. I know many of you reading these words need to understand because you are praying for things and waiting on things that could have a drastic impact on your life. God is waiting for you to let go of it and put your focus back on him. Somewhere along the way you lost your focus on God and your prayers have been out of alignment ever since. He is waiting on *you*.

When I think of all of my prayers and all the times I have waited on God for things, I am more thankful for the prayers that God did not answer than the ones he did. My life and my joy is just as much a result of unanswered prayer as it is answered prayer.

For some of you this Advent season may not be about waiting; it may be about God waiting on you. Amen.

Advent 3
John 1:6-8, 19-28

There was a man sent from God, whose name was John. He came as a witness to testify to the light, so that all might believe through him. He himself was not the light, but he came to testify to the light. This is the testimony given by John when the Jews sent priests and Levites from Jerusalem to ask him, "Who are you?" He confessed and did not deny it, but confessed, "I am not the Messiah." And they asked him, "What then? Are you Elijah?" He said, "I am not." "Are you the prophet?" He answered, "No." Then they said to him, "Who are you? Let us have an answer for those who sent us. What do you say about yourself?" He said, "I am the voice of one crying out in the wilderness, 'Make straight the way of the Lord,'" as the prophet Isaiah said. Now they had been sent from the Pharisees. They asked him, "Why then are you baptizing if you are neither the Messiah, nor Elijah, nor the prophet?" John answered them, "I baptize with water. Among you stands one whom you do not know, the one who is coming after me; I am not worthy to untie the thong of his sandal." This took place in Bethany across the Jordan where John was baptizing.

A Light in the Darkness

(after the Newtown, Connecticut, school shooting)
    I was finishing up my sermon on a Friday when my
phone buzzed with the horrific news of the tragedy at Sandy
Hook Elementary. As I watched the news unfold, I knew the
message I had prepared would not be adequate. I knew a different message would need to be preached. I believe you will
understand why I will be going in a different direction today.
We were shocked, we were angry, we were afraid, we were
heartbroken, and I must speak to that today.
    I have cried several times over that tragedy, as I know
many of you have. That was the only appropriate way to
begin to respond to that unthinkable and unspeakable event.
Children, anticipating the joy of Christmas, were taken from
us — innocent children who had their whole lives ahead of
them, all their hopes and dreams were gone in an instant.
    We cried for the parents and family of those lost. We
cried for the community of Newtown, Connecticut, that was
going through unimaginable and unbearable grief. As we
cried, we hugged our children a little tighter and we told
each other "I love you" a little more. We also recognized
how precious life really is.
    If we are honest, we were also angry. We were like the Old
Testament prophets who shouted out with anger and indig-
nation at the evil in this world. The governor of Connecticut
was right when he said, "Evil has visited this town…" We
were angry at this evil and we railed against it.
    Our grief and anger eventually gave way to prayer. We
prayed to God with our questions, our anger, our grief, and

our despair — "Lord, how could this happen? Lord, why did this happen? Lord, is there a word from you in all of this? Lord, the world is so dark, so violent, so bloody, so hateful! Lord, may your kingdom come, now! Why is there a delay to your kingdom, O Lord? When will your kingdom come, O Lord?"

I want to address the questions that many of us prayed then and now — the questions we struggle with. I know all of us come here today with questions we want answered. Our hearts cry out with questions because these kinds of tragedies shatter our ideas of how the world is supposed to operate.

I remember several years ago when a man named Mark Barton walked into an Atlanta business office and shot and killed people. The next day the *Atlanta Constitution* carried a poignant cartoon of a little boy sitting next to his mother on the couch. There was a newspaper on the coffee table that showed the headline: "Atlanta Murderer: Mark Barton." The boy looked up at his mother and said, "You said monsters don't exist."

Well, that pretty much sums it up, doesn't it? How many children right now are asking, "Mommy, Daddy I thought you said monsters don't exist?" How many of us adults are asking the same question in different ways: "Why do these evil things exist? Why would God allow these tragedies that have broken America's heart? Why did God allow twenty children to be killed? Why did God allow a principal who cared so much about education to be taken from us? Why did God allow a school psychologist who loved children so much to be killed? Why didn't God divert the shooter? Why didn't God intervene?" People have asked me these questions many times. What is the answer?

The answer is one word — freedom. We live in a world where God has given us freedom. The same freedom that allows us to choose to love and serve God allows others to pick up weapons and kill innocent people. Freedom itself is good, like all of God's gifts, but some choose to pervert God's gift and use it for evil. Why didn't God intervene? Why didn't God do something to prevent this? Because freedom was at stake. Jim Somerville expressed it well, "If God took away our freedom to do evil he would also be taking away our freedom to do good!" If God did that we would just be a bunch of numb robots incapable of love or hate.

God wraps his loving arms around the victims of these tragedies and around a broken and devastated nation. God's heart is torn apart as he sees his gift of freedom being perverted repeatedly.

We hold on to the hope that one day God's kingdom will be fully realized on earth and God will wipe every tear. Fear, violence, hatred, war, and bloodshed will be no more! Until that day comes we have to cope with tragedies like these. How do we do it? We cope by understanding where God is in the midst of tragedy.

So where is God in the midst of these tragedies? This question underscores the importance of Advent. We have a tendency to romanticize Advent — when Christ was born all was clean — all was majestic — all was calm and silent — all was bright. No, it wasn't! This is not the world Christ was born into. He was born rejected in a smelly, messy, rat-infested feeding trough for animals in the small town of Bethlehem. When Jesus was born, King Herod felt so threatened he commanded all little boys two and under in and around Bethlehem to be slaughtered. Jesus was born in the midst of the mass murder of children.

God did not connect with this world from afar with angels surrounding him singing the *Hallelujah* chorus. God became flesh in the midst of our ugly and messy lives. Advent means there is no place so dark, dirty, or ugly that God will not go to be with us, to love us, to understand us, to comfort us, to save us, and to redeem us! Only the Christian faith dares to claim that God emptied himself completely and went through the entire human experience. God gets down beside us to feel our pain and to heal our lives.

Isaiah 40:11 (NIV) says, "He gathers the lambs in his arms and carries them close to his heart." You want to know where those precious children are? God gathered those lambs close to him and said: "Don't you worry. They are in the safest place imaginable. I have tucked them close to my heart and I will never let them go."

Where was God on that Friday morning of the Connecticut shooting? He was holding the victims, feeling the pain of their wounds. Where was God? He was wailing with the parents in the churches. Where was God? He was wailing and crying with our nation. And as God cried with us I believe he said: "How long will my children do this to each other? How long will this precious world of mine choose such evil and destruction? How long?" Oh, the patience and long-suffering of almighty God!

It does not escape us that we even killed God when he came upon this earth. He conquered death, but what do we think the cross means? As God in Christ is on the cross he cries out, "When will the world learn that my love is the answer? Not more violence — not more war — not more political rhetoric — not more arguments — not more policies — not more technology! How much clearer can I make it?"

So where is God? He is right here, closer than our breath, tasting our tears, loving us eternally. Because we know that God is near we can respond to these tragedies.

We can respond by showing the world the light of Christ that overcomes the darkness. Isn't that what Christmas is all about? John 1:9 (NIV) states, "The true light that gives light to every man was coming into the world." The same light that was in Christ lives in each of us. This is why we need Christmas now more than ever! "What has come into being

34

in him was life, and the life was the light of all people. The light shines in the darkness, and the darkness did not overcome it" (John 1:3-5).

Do you know what these powerful words from the gospel of John mean right now? They mean when the world is at its worst, the church needs to be at her best! Where are the devastated people flocking to? The church! What other institution can offer hope, light, love, strength, and faith in the midst of tragedy? What other institution can do what the church can do? We are the light!

It is in the midst of tragedies like this that we must relearn the lesson that we don't draw people to Christ by being judgmental, self-righteous, ecclesiastical, and spiritually arrogant. We don't draw people to Christ by telling others we are right and they are wrong. "We draw people to Christ" said Madeleine L'Engle, "by reflecting a light that is so lovely and compelling that they want with all of their hearts to know the source of it."

The message of Advent is that God's light is stronger than the darkness, God's love is stronger than hate, and God's power is stronger than death. How will the world know unless we show them? We have a nation filled with broken and hurting people who are wondering, "Where is God? Is this all there is to life — killing, hate, violence, and bloodshed? Is this all there is?" How will the world know any different unless we show them the light? That is your job this week and that is my job this week. We are to take the light that is in here and carry it with us — to our work places, homes, neighborhoods — to the grocery stores and shops we visit. Let Jesus' light shine through you! If there is to be peaceful change in this world, it begins in each of us!

When Mister Rogers was a boy and saw frightening things in the news, his mother would say something very wise to him. She would say, "Look for the helpers. You will always find people who are helping." We need to do the same. We need to be encouraged by all the helpers. In fact, all the helpers should be a motivator for us to join them. Let us be the helpers! Let us be the light and show the world that the light of Christ is stronger than the darkness.

Haven't we seen so many amazing people who are sharing the light? What about Robbie Parker, the father of Emilie Parker who was killed in the Sandy Hook shooting? This wonderful man of faith had the courage to give a national interview. He spoke of the love and innocence of his precious daughter and how much he loved being her father. When a reporter asked how he was going to move on, he replied, "I'm going to move on by helping as many people as I can." Robbie Parker chose to let his light shine!

There was also first-grade teacher Kaitlin Roig who heard what sounded like the rapid firing of an assault rifle. "I knew something was wrong," she told ABC "World News" anchor Diane Sawyer. She rushed the fourteen children, aged six and seven, into the class bathroom. She helped some climb onto the toilet so they could all fit in the tiny room. Then she locked the door. "I just told them we had to be absolutely quiet," Roig told Sawyer. "If they started crying, I would take their face and tell them, 'I love you. It's going to be okay.' I wanted that to be the last thing they heard, not the gunfire in the hall."

When she said "I told them I loved them," isn't that what God wants us to hear? Not the gunfire, but the love. Listen, even in our darkest hour of need God has us in his arms and he whispers, "I love you and nothing can separate you from my love." It is the strongest power in the world.

How do we respond? We do something that Jesus said to his disciples and it is something many of us have heard, but we are skeptical that it will really work. The truth is that it is the only thing that will heal our world. What is it? You know it. Jesus said, "I give you a new commandment, that you love one another. Just as I have loved you" (John 13:34).

This love is what will heal you, me, this country, and this world.

"The light shines in the darkness, and the darkness did not overcome it" (John 1:5).

Let us pray:
O Lord, our hearts break with your heart when we hear the news of children and adults killed at schools. We cry out with fear, anger, and despair. Lord, comfort those who have lost loved ones. Strengthen law enforcement officers and public officials. We also pray for the family of the perpetrators. This is Advent, the season where we celebrate your light coming into this dark world and your love becoming flesh in the midst of our mess. We need you to come once again and enable us to reflect your light so the world will know that you are stronger than death and more loving than hate and nothing will be able to separate us from you. Amen.

Advent 4
Luke 1:26-38

In the sixth month the angel Gabriel was sent by God to a town in Galilee called Nazareth, to a virgin engaged to a man whose name was Joseph, of the house of David. The virgin's name was Mary. And he came to her and said, "Greetings, favored one! The Lord is with you." But she was much perplexed by his words and pondered what sort of greeting this might be. The angel said to her, "Do not be afraid, Mary, for you have found favor with God. And now, you will conceive in your womb and bear a son, and you will name him Jesus. He will be great, and will be called the Son of the Most High, and the Lord God will give to him the throne of his ancestor David. He will reign over the house of Jacob forever, and of his kingdom there will be no end." Mary said to the angel, "How can this be, since I am a virgin?" The angel said to her, "The Holy Spirit will come upon you, and the power of the Most High will overshadow you; therefore the child to be born will be holy; he will be called Son of God. And now, your relative Elizabeth in her old age has also conceived a son; and this is the sixth month for her who was said to be barren. For nothing will be impossible with God." Then Mary said, "Here am I, the servant of the Lord; let it be with me according to your word." Then the angel departed from her.

Nothing Is Impossible
with God!

To me the best thing about Christmas is the surprises. Who does not enjoy the look of wondrous surprise on a child's face on Christmas morning? Who among us does not remember the rush of excitement we experienced when we were surprised on Christmas day with the best gift ever?

I will always remember the surprise I experienced the Christmas of 1984. That Christmas I received one of the best gifts an American boy could receive. In the months leading up to Christmas I had begged my parents for it, but they didn't seem too keen on giving it to me. I had resigned myself to the fact that I was not going to get it. When I came down the stairs on Christmas morning, my doubts seemed to be confirmed. There was no gift that matched the size and shape of the gift I wanted. Toward the end of our chaotic unwrapping session, I noticed a box hidden under other gifts. It had my name on it. I opened it up and there was a note that read, "Go to the garage to see what this goes with!" In the box was a blue helmet! I ran to the garage door and opened it, and there it was in all of its glory — a bright blue shiny go-cart! Surprise! I almost heard angels singing!

Christmas is all about surprises. In fact, Christmas began with a big surprise. Mary got the biggest surprise of her life when the angel Gabriel appeared to her and told her that she would be pregnant with the Son of God! What could be more astonishing than that? Maybe "shocked" is a better word. After all, she was a virgin. Surprise!

Christmas is about the joyous surprises of God. In the spirit of the surprise of Christmas I want to open up a few Christmas surprises from Mary's story because through Mary's story we find the transforming message of Christmas. If you take that message to heart you will never be the same.

If there is one thing Mary's surprise teaches us it is that God loves to do extraordinary things through ordinary people. Mary was just a poor, Jewish teenage girl. Based on life expectancy at the time Mary was probably between the ages of thirteen and sixteen. Mary didn't have much experience in life. She was not sophisticated. Yet, God chose her to birth the Son of God.

Luke reports that Mary was "perplexed" by what the angel told her (Luke 1:29). This is perhaps the greatest understatement in the Bible. If an angel appeared to you, would "perplexed" be the best word to describe your reaction? No, you would be terrified! So was Mary! Gabriel sensed Mary's fear and explained why he was appearing to her. Mary's response in verse 34 was priceless, "How can this be?" In our vernacular, Mary asked, "Are you kidding me? How is that going to happen? Um, there is a problem here. I am a virgin. How can this be?"

Many of us have the same reaction when God desires to birth something great through us. We are perplexed. We can't bring ourselves to believe it. We are afraid. We have doubts. We have excuses. "How can this be?"

Maybe for a long time God has been tugging on your heart to do an extraordinary thing and you have given every excuse in the book why you are not able to do it. God wants you to do it and all *you* can give God back are your doubts and excuses. "I'm too old. I'm too young. I'm not smart enough. I'm not good enough. I'm not educated enough. I'm not experienced enough. How can this be?" If that is where you are today, it is time to get the word "can't" out of your vocabulary.

Look at what Mary said to the angel in Luke 1:38. After the angel explained that all this was going to happen through the power of the Holy Spirit, Mary stepped out in faith and said, "Here am I, a servant of the Lord, let it be according to God's word!" Mary moved beyond her doubts and excuses and said "yes" to God! Aren't we glad she did?

Mary believed in herself and believed in God. She was used by God in a powerful way. But what exactly turned the key for Mary? Why caused her to move beyond her doubts? I believe it was what the angel Gabriel said to Mary in verse 37, "For nothing is impossible with God!"

Mary knew this. Mary believed this. Otherwise, she could not have done what she did. Imagine the fears and doubts she had to overcome. All Mary knew were the risks. For example, can you imagine how Joseph reacted when Mary told him that she was pregnant with Son of God? "Right, Mary. Sure. Some spirit got you pregnant." In fact, Joseph was making plans to quietly leave until God got a hold of him. What's more is that Mary knew that she risked being ostracized by her family and community. She risked rejection. She risked being humiliated.

Yet, knowing all that and risking all that, Mary said "yes" to God because she believed that nothing was impossible with God! She believed God would do what he said he would do.

Do you want to know how to be used by God for a great purpose? It is revealed later through something Elizabeth said to her cousin Mary when they met. Elizabeth said to Mary, "And blessed is she who *believed* that there would be a fulfillment of what was spoken to her by the Lord" (Luke 1:45, emphasis added).

Matthew Hartsfield reminds us to notice what Elizabeth did *not* say. She did not say, "Mary, you are blessed because you come from the right family. Mary, you are blessed because you are beautiful. Mary, you are blessed because you are intelligent. Mary, you are blessed because you are so-phisticated." No! Mary was blessed because she believed God would do what he said he would.

God does not bless us because of our ability; God blesses us because of our availability. We see this confirmed throughout the Bible. Have you ever taken a look at the people God uses? Most of them belong on the island of the "Lost and Misfit Toys" yet God did powerful things through all of them simply because they were available. Are you available? God blesses and uses us to the fullest when we say, "Lord, I make myself available to you. Use me however you want to use me. Do your will in my life."

You see, Mary got this. Mary got that it wasn't about her. It was about what God could do through her. This is revealed in the greatest Christmas carol ever written. Think for a moment. What do you think is the greatest Christmas carol ever written? "Silent Night?" "Joy To The World?" "White Christmas?" "Rudolph The Red-Nosed Reindeer?" John Ortberg reminds us that the greatest Christmas carol was written by a Jewish peasant girl named Mary over 2,000 years ago. It is called "The Magnificat." It is the beautiful words she pours forth to God beginning in verse 46. In "The Magnificat" all Mary can do is talk about what God has done.

When we stop thinking about our limitations and begin believing in what God can do through us, life begins to open up for us. When we stop trying to control our lives and say, "God, you take it from here," real life begins.

There is a touching verse in "The Magnificat." It is verse 48. Mary said, "For he has looked with favor on the lowliness of his servant." Other translations say, "He has been mindful." The one I like the best, which I believe best describes Mary's experience is "He has taken notice." Can't you feel Mary's emotion? "God, you have taken notice of me — a poor teenage girl. You have taken notice of me!"

If there is one consistent theme throughout the Bible it is that God loves us and takes notice of each of us. Now that sounds simple enough, but you would not believe how difficult it is to convince people that it is true. As a preacher, I hear so many myths about God. When I am on the golf course and people find out I am a preacher they will give me a four foot putt and say things like, "Be sure to say a good word about me to the man upstairs. I'd like to get into heaven. I have been a bad boy." Or they will say, "You seem nice, but I could never go to church. Lightning would strike."

What does John 3:16 say? Hartsfield reminds us again to look at what this verse does not say. It does not say, "God so loved the perfect people." It does not say, "God so loved the religious people." It says, "For God so loved the world!"

Receive God's love today. God takes notice of you and cares for you. What do we think Christmas is all about? Love came down at Christmas to show each of us that God takes notice of us and wants to be in our lives. God wants to redeem us with his grace, encourage us with his love, guide us with his wisdom, and use us with his power.

Don't listen to your doubts. Don't listen to what the critics say. Listen to what God says about you and what God wants to do through you. No one ever did anything great for God by listening to criticism.

Have you ever heard the story about Jan Paderewski, the great concert pianist? When he was young he left Poland to play his first recital in London. Before he left, he asked an influential musician to give him a letter of introduction to a leading figure in Britain's musical world who might be able to help Paderewski if he was not able to live up to his dreams. The letter was handed to him in a sealed envelope. He hoped that he would accomplish everything he set out to do and would not have to use the letter. Fortunately, he never had to use it. He was an instant success. Some years later, while going through his papers, he came upon the letter and opened it. It read: "This will introduce Jan Paderewski, who plays the piano, for which he demonstrates no conspicuous talent."[1]

What if Paderewski had opened the letter in the beginning? He may not have believed that he had the gift God had blessed him with. He may not have performed that first recital. He may not have become who he was created to become!

What if Mary had listened to her doubts instead of listening to God? The world would be a different place.

Did you know that God wants to do something extraordinary through you? Did you know that nothing is impossible with God? Did you know that God takes notice of you? That is the message of Christmas and if you believe it, it will change your life. Amen.

---

1. *Bits and Pieces*, January 9, 1992, pp. 1-2.

Christmas Eve / Day
Luke 2:1-14 (15-20)

In those days a decree went out from Emperor Augustus that all the world should be registered. This was the first registration and was taken while Quirinius was governor of Syria. All went to their own towns to be registered. Joseph also went from the town of Nazareth in Galilee to Judea, to the city of David called Bethlehem, because he was descended from the house and family of David.... When the angels had left them and gone into heaven, the shepherds said to one another, "Let us go now to Bethlehem and see this thing that has taken place, which the Lord has made known to us." So they went with haste and found Mary and Joseph, and the child lying in the manger. When they saw this, they made known what had been told them about this child; and all who heard it were amazed at what the shepherds told them. But Mary treasured all these words and pondered them in her heart. The shepherds returned, glorifying and praising God for all they had heard and seen, as it had been told them.

The Joy of Christmas

One of my favorite Christmas stories is about the young boy who was given a very important role in the church Christmas play. He was to be the angel and announce the birth of Jesus. For weeks he rehearsed the line that had been given to him, "Behold, I bring you good news of great joy!"

The grandparents got in on it and any time the family was together and the boy was there they would dress him up in his costume and he would rehearse his part for them, "Behold, I bring you good news of great joy." They were certain that when he grew up he would be another Charlton Heston.

The great night came for the Christmas pageant and everybody was in place. All the grandparents and extended family were there. Visitors had come in and all the children were in costumes, complete with bathrobes for the three kings and fake wings and halos for the angels. All the mothers were excited and everyone was really into this.

As the pageant started, the excitement was electric around the room. The dramatic event in the first part was the announcement of the angel, "Behold, I bring you good news of great joy." The spotlight hit this young boy and as he stood center stage in the middle of all this excitement he got stage fright. Every grandparent, aunt, uncle, and neighbor came to the edge of their seats, wanting to say it for him. You could see them in unison, mouthing, "Behold, I bring you good news of great joy."

Still, his brain was frozen; he couldn't say it. He tried it, but it just wouldn't come. Finally, in a courageous moment he filled his lungs with breath and blurted out the words, "Have I got news for you!"[1]

The boy got it right. Do we have great news or what? At Christmas we celebrate the coming of our Lord and Savior Jesus Christ. Christmas means that we don't search for God; God searches for us. Christmas means that God put skin on to show us how much he cares for us. Christmas means that God became one of us in Christ so that we would understand the depth of his love and be changed by it. And if this is not great news, I don't know what is!

I want us to get back to the joy of Christmas. I want the message to penetrate our lives and our hearts. I want us to look beyond the glitter and wrapping and get to the real gift of Christmas. I want us to throw away our pre-conceived notions about this time of year and be transformed by Christmas.

How do we do it? Our text in Luke gives us some clues, and it is all about the shepherds. I believe the shepherds in our text give us the key to finding the joy of Christmas.

What is it about the shepherds that is so special? At the time of Jesus, shepherds were considered the lowest rung in society. They were dirty. They did not bathe very much. It was not acceptable to associate with them. Back then a common prayer was "Please, don't let my child be a shepherd." Why would God reveal his message to shepherds? Why would God choose to tell the shepherds first?

God chose to reveal the gift of Christmas first to the shepherds because they were the most receptive to the message. They did not have anything to prove. They had no reputation to protect. They had no fear of being called crazy. More than anyone they were open to the impossible — God was being born among them!

What did the shepherds have that no one else had? What did they possess that gave them this ability? What can they teach us about how to be impacted by the joy of Christmas? One thing we notice is that the shepherds had eyes to see.

After they had heard from the angels, they said, "Let's go to Bethlehem and *see* what has taken place..." They got there and saw the scene. It was not spectacular. To any other eye it was worse than ordinary, but the shepherds were amazed. They were able to see Christ.

Most of us don't see this well. We see what we want to see. We go about our lives passing by holy events and we don't even notice. We rush through life and are unaware of where Christ is in our midst. We walk right by situations where God is active and working. We just don't see it.

The great landscape artist Joseph Turner was known for painting very vivid landscapes. They were filled with color and imagery. They looked alive. One time an art critic approached Turner and said, "Your paintings are so vivid, but I have never seen landscapes look like that." Turner replied, "Yes, but don't you wish you could?"

I imagine when the shepherds told others about what they saw there were some who replied, "How could you see something like that? We have never seen anything like that!" Perhaps the shepherds said, "Don't you wish you could?"

If there is one thing I want for Christmas it is for everyone to see what the shepherds saw, that Christ is the Savior of the world — the whole wide world. Not just for America, but for everyone — red, yellow, black, white, we are all precious in his sight. If peace, hope, love, and joy are to come to this world, we must have the eyes to see that Jesus is the Christ, the Savior of the whole world. The Bible says that every knee shall bow and every tongue will confess that Jesus Christ is Lord!

We also notice that the shepherds had ears to hear. The shepherds heard the angels singing but not everyone heard it — just the shepherds. They were in the fields, far enough away from the bustle of the city to hear the sacred sounds.

We live in a noisy world. Just stop for a moment during your day and listen to all the noise around you. We get so used to noise that we can't stand silence. The sad thing is that most of the noise we hear drowns out the sacred sounds, the real sounds, the holy of sounds of God. There is so much noise that we don't hear very well. If we want to hear from God, we must find the silence that the shepherds found.

I like the story about Franklin Delano Roosevelt. One day he was tired of all the small talk during receptions at the White House. As a long line of people were waiting to shake his hand he decided to say, "I killed my mother-in-law last night." People did not hear it. They walked by and said, "That's nice." Then a foreign diplomat came through and FDR said, "I killed my mother-in-law last night." The diplomat replied, "And I am sure she deserved it!"

There was once a Native American and a native New Yorker walking the streets of New York City together. The Native American spent his whole life on the prairie. It was his first time in the city. He turned to his new friend and said, "I hear a cricket." The New Yorker replied, "What do you mean? Look at the asphalt, smell the exhaust, look at the tall buildings. How can there be a cricket here?"

The Native American led his friend across the street to the front of a store. There in front of the store was a small tree. He turned over a leaf and there was a cricket. The Native American said, "We hear what we are trained to hear. Let me show you." He took change out of his pocket and threw it on the street and a crowd of people stopped.

We hear what we want to hear. We see what we want to see. We respond how we choose to respond. In order for us to hear and receive the power of Christ and Christmas we must move away from our distractions and listen.

Most of all we recognize that the shepherds had the courage to commit. Later in our passage the shepherds went back, praised God, and told everyone what they had seen. By doing so, they decided to believe. They decided to proclaim at the risk of looking foolish. They decided to commit. They were so filled with joy they could not contain it. They had to share it.

We live in a crazy world that does not like to commit to anything. Joseph Bella, a sociologist, wrote a book titled *Habits of the Heart*. In the book he analyzes America and he says that the symbolic city of America is not New York or Washington but Las Vegas.

He writes about a survey he did where he asked Americans what they believed. The most consistent result was that they did not want to commit themselves. He writes about doing a survey with a girl named Sheila. She said, "I don't want to commit. I just want to feel good all the time about where I am and what I am doing."

Bella says America is covered in Sheilas. Today, our culture is known for its Sheilaism. No one wants to commit to anything. Folks wonder why they never change, why they never experience life the way they want to. Folks wonder why they have no joy. Joy can only be found by committing to the love of Christ and the purpose Christ has for your life.

Christmas is just a nice concert easily forgotten unless we embrace Jesus' love for us and commit to him. Until we commit to the Christ in Christmas, life is just an endless and boring series of experiences and obligations. We will not see. We will not hear. We will not find joy until we decide to commit. We will not have the joy, hope, peace, and love that we hunger for until we commit. Ann Weems said it best: "If Christmas is not now, if Christ is not born into the everyday present, then what is all the noise about?" Indeed, if there is no commitment in us, what is all the noise about?

There is an ancient Christmas legend that tells of how God called the angels of heaven together one day for a special choir rehearsal. God told the angelic choir that he wanted them to learn a special song for a very special occasion. The angels got very excited and they rehearsed the song for weeks.

God was quite demanding of his choir but the angels assumed it was for a very good reason.

Finally, God felt that they were ready to sing the song but before they did he had one important thing to tell them — they would only perform the song once. Some of the angels complained. They just didn't understand. The song was so beautiful and they sang it so well. Why sing it only once? God told to his angels to trust him and later they would understand.

One night God called the angels together and said, "It's time." He led them to a field just outside of Bethlehem and the angels sang their song. And boy did they sing it! "Glory to God in the highest and on earth peace and good will toward all." As the angels sang, they began to understand the significance of the song and why they were singing it. The song was announcing the birth of the Savior of the world!

When the angels finished singing, God led them back to heaven and reminded them that they would not sing that song again as an angelic choir. They could hum the song occasionally as individuals but they would never perform it again. One angel was overcome with curiosity and courageously asked God why they could not sing that majestic anthem again. They did it so well. It felt so right. Why couldn't they sing that great song anymore? "Because," God explained, "my Son has been born and now earth must do the singing."[2]

Will you sing? God is waiting. A Savior has been born. Amen.

---

1. Tom Long, *Something Is About to Happen* (Lima, Ohio: CSS Publishing Company, Inc., 1996), p. 7.

2. James Moore, *Let Us Go Over to Bethlehem* (Nashville: Abingdon Press, 2001), p. 18.

Christmas 1
Luke 2:22-40

When the time came for their purification according to the law of Moses, they brought him up to Jerusalem to present him to the Lord (as it is written in the law of the Lord, "Every firstborn male shall be designated as holy to the Lord"), and they offered a sacrifice according to what is stated in the law of the Lord, "a pair of turtledoves or two young pigeons." Now there was a man in Jerusalem whose name was Simeon; this man was righteous and devout, looking forward to the consolation of Israel, and the Holy Spirit rested on him. It had been revealed to him by the Holy Spirit that he would not see death before he had seen the Lord's Messiah. Guided by the Spirit, Simeon came into the temple; and when the parents brought in the child Jesus, to do for him what was customary under the law, Simeon took him in his arms and praised God, saying, "Master, now you are dismissing your servant in peace, according to your word; for my eyes have seen your salvation, which you have prepared in the presence of all peoples, a light for revelation to the Gentiles and for glory to your people Israel." And the child's father and mother were amazed at what was being said about him. Then Simeon blessed them and said to his mother Mary, "This child is destined for the falling and the rising of many in Israel, and to be a sign that will be opposed so that the inner thoughts of many will be revealed — and a sword will pierce your own soul too." There was also a prophet, Anna the daughter of Phanuel, of the tribe of Asher. She was of a great age, having lived with her husband seven years after her marriage, then as a widow to the age of eighty-four. She never left the temple but worshiped there with fasting and prayer night and day. At that moment she came, and began to praise God and to speak about the child to all who were

*looking for the redemption of Jerusalem. When they had fin-
ished everything required by the law of the Lord, they returned to Galilee, to their own town of Nazareth. The child
grew and became strong, filled with wisdom; and the favor
of God was upon him.*

The Power of Patience

Let's be honest. Many folks have a strong faith in God and are seeking his will in everything they do, but they are still waiting on God to answer their prayers. They could be praying for a new job, a relationship, an illness, a problem at work, or a personal struggle. They have prayed repeatedly and have sought God's will and still there is no answer, no sign, no movement. Maybe you know someone like that?

Perhaps that someone is you. If you are honest, you are growing really impatient with God. You don't get it. You have done everything you are supposed to — brought your need to God, prayed faithfully, examined your heart, and the bottom line is you have a need, a problem, an issue, a desire, and there is still no answer from God. You are discouraged and getting ready to give up on your prayers and maybe even give up on your faith.

Don't give up. Don't quit on your prayers. Don't quit seeking God. The message I have will give you encouragement and inspiration. This message will help you move beyond your discouragement by seeing that there is wisdom in waiting. In fact, this message will motivate you to stop watching the clock and start getting yourself prepared for God's answer! God will answer your prayer, count on that!

I know some of you find this hard to believe. Mr. Right or Mrs. Right has not shown up. You are still stuck in the same tired situation. That problem at work doesn't seem to ever go away. That personal struggle in your life just doesn't stop. You can't see your life changing for the better. You think your life is going to be more of the same forever and ever. You think you will have to live with failure and disappointment.

The good news is that Christmas is all about preparing ourselves for God to enter our lives in a powerful way. We set aside this season every year not just to decorate the trees, give and receive gifts, sing the carols and drink hot chocolate, but to prepare ourselves for God's perfect answer to our problems, our struggles, our pain, our disappointments, and our frustration with waiting.

Look at Simeon. He had been waiting for years for the birth of Christ. He prayed for the moment he could hold Christ in his arms and praise God for providing a Savior for the world. God had promised it. He told Simeon to keep waiting patiently and Christ would be born. Simeon was faithful. He never lost faith in God. He waited with trust. The day finally came. Joseph and Mary brought Jesus into the temple and Simeon took him in his arms and gave thanks to God for keeping his promise. Christ was born! The light had come and the darkness would never overcome it.

When Joseph brought his child into the temple I am sure he resonated with Simeon's relief and gratitude to God. He, like Simeon, understood what it felt like to seek God for an answer and have to wait for it. But after he experienced what God promised he was never the same again.

The irony is that Joseph is kind of the stepchild in the Christmas story. He always takes a backseat to Mary, the angels, and the wise men. When I was a child I played Joseph in our church's Christmas program. I was all excited. I got my perfect bathrobe ready. I was ready to repeat my lines with perfection. I went to my first rehearsal and was disappointed to find that Joseph only had one line! That was it! One line! My line was a question to the innkeeper, "Do you have a room available?" The rest of the time I was just supposed to stand there next to the crummy animals and look happy! Poor Joseph always gets the short end of the stick.

But Joseph's story is a powerful one that can teach us the wisdom and power of waiting on God. If we take a closer look at what he did and the role he played in the Christmas story, we will find a message that can make a huge difference to our faith.

Most of us know the story of Christmas and most of us know the role Joseph played in the story but in order to see the power in it let me tell you what happened. Joseph and Mary met. Sparks flew. Joseph proposed to Mary and she accepted. They were engaged! Engagement back then meant a lot more than a sparkling rock and a promise. Both families went to their lawyers and signed an agreement. You could get out of the engagement but it took a lot of red tape.

Mary got sick one morning and Joseph noticed that something wasn't right. Mary 'fessed up. She told Joseph she was pregnant. That would have been bad enough because they both came from very religious families, but they had bigger problems. Joseph was not the father because they had not been together before marriage! Joseph asked, "Who is the father?" This is when the soap opera fades out for a commercial!

The story continued as Mary told Joseph that she had not been with any other man. He said, "Well Mary how did it happen? Did a stork come?" Mary dropped the bomb on Joseph and told him that the child in her was conceived by the Holy Spirit. Now, honestly, if you had been Joseph, would you have believed her? "Really, Mary? So I am supposed to believe this? Sure. You need to get your head examined. Have you lost your mind?" This is better than a soap opera! What happens next is really interesting. Matthew 1:19 (NIV) reads:

> Because Joseph her husband was a righteous man and did not want to expose her to public disgrace, he had in mind to divorce her quietly.

According to the law, it was Joseph's right to have Mary stoned to death! She had shamed him and shamed the family. But he was a good religious man so he decided to do the most humane thing, just divorce her quietly, sign the papers, and go back to match.com to find another wife. But look at what happened next in Matthew 1:20-21 (NIV):

> But after he had considered this, an angel of the Lord appeared to him in a dream and said, "Joseph son of David, do not be afraid to take Mary home as your wife, because what is conceived in her is from the Holy Spirit. She will give birth to a son, and you are to give him the name Jesus, because he will save his people from their sins."

Joseph woke up and said, "I must have had too much wine last night. This can't be true! Did that really happen?" You know how dreams are. You never know. But something inside Joseph decided to trust God, to believe that the dream was true. Look at verse 24 (NIV):

> When Joseph woke up, he did what the angel of the Lord had commanded him and took Mary home as his wife.

It's a wonderful story. Joseph decided to take Mary as his wife! What I want to focus on is the time between Joseph making this decision and Jesus being born — the time Joseph had to wait. We don't hear anything about this but I believe those nine months Joseph had to wait were the most pivotal nine months of his life. Can you imagine how many times he doubted his decision and thought of bolting? "I'm basing all of this on a dream! What if when this child is born he looks like the milkman? Look at the way my friends and family look at me in public. They don't believe me. I can tell. I wouldn't believe me either! What a crazy idea. Am I really doing this?" Can you imagine how many times Joseph doubted God and thought of making a decision he thought was right for him, like leaving Mary?

I know many of you are in that boat. You have been waiting and waiting. You trusted God in the beginning but your patience is wearing thin. The trust you had is leaking. You are afraid. You are angry. You are confused. You think you are all alone. You think God has abandoned you and your prayers. You are sick and tired of waiting and you are ready to make a quick decision that you think is best.

Hold on. Let me remind you what happened to Joseph. After waiting nine months and worrying, doubting, and probably thinking about leaving Mary, his son Jesus was born. The star in the east lit up the sky. The angels sang like heaven. The Magi came. The dream was true! His son was the Christ! Imagine Joseph's satisfaction. Imagine how good he felt for waiting, for trusting God, for being patient! Imagine Joseph being at a dinner party and people are introducing themselves and what they do. They are bragging. Joseph is just sitting there very quiet. He is waiting his turn and politely listening. Finally, it is his turn, "My name is Joseph. I'm a carpenter. I'm married to Mary. Oh, and I'm also the father of the Savior of the world!"

I tell you this because I know there are many of you who are in the waiting period that Joseph was in before the dream became a reality. You are in that period between trusting God and getting your prayers answered. You are in that period between believing and receiving and some of you are about to give up hope. Some of you already have. You are tired of waiting on God. You think all this time of waiting has been a waste of time. You have lost your patience and you are ready to do what is convenient and what seems right to you.

I want you to pause right now. Push the pause button and think of Joseph. Just think what he would have missed if he had decided to leave Mary. Just think how that would have altered his life and the destiny God had for him. He would have missed rearing and nurturing the Savior of the world! He would have missed being one of the most important figures in the history of the world. But he didn't miss it because he was patient.

I don't want you to miss God's wonderful plan for you! Don't quit on your faith. Don't take the easy road. Don't rush into something you will regret. God is working his purpose out for you. He is doing things in your present right now that will affect your future. This is why your patience and trust of God is critical! What we often think is waiting is part of God's larger plan. Don't spoil God's best for you. Remember this: Patience is resisting the immediate to receive God's best.

We often hear "the devil is in the details." No, God is in the details! That is why your patience with God and your trust in him is critical. You don't know the things he is working out in the midst of your waiting to bring an answer to you that may be even better than you imagined. This time of waiting needs to be a time of listening and preparing for God's best for you — a relationship, a new job, a new calling, a different path, a new desire, a new birth like Joseph received, a totally unexpected situation that is beyond your imagination! God's ways are higher than our ways! Patience is resisting the immediate to receive God's best.

Vic Pentz shared a story that is one of the most powerful examples of how God is in the details. Pentz had a parishioner in his church who was a manager at Microsoft. He prayed and prayed that somehow his life could make a difference to someone. He was growing in his faith but he was disillusioned at work. He was well paid but he felt he wasn't making any difference. He was getting restless and thought of quitting his job. He spoke to a mentor at work who he trusted about his dilemma. His mentor suggested that he hold off on quitting his job and told him, "Why don't you get to know the people who work for you? Instead of emailing and texting people who sit just ten feet away from you, get up and go speak with them, you know, like they matter!"

A few weeks later one of his employees walked into his office and gave him a brand new Xbox gaming system. He knew what he paid the guy and it wasn't much so he asked, "How did you get the money to buy this?" He said, "I sold my gun." He said, "What?" He said, "Yeah you see six months ago my mom died and I got really depressed. I thought of killing myself. So I bought a gun and held that gun every night and contemplated doing it. I knew no one would miss me. The only way you would know is if payroll notified you. But then you did something you had never done before. You came out of your office and patted me on the back and told me that my emails made you laugh and that you really appreciate the good work I do because it makes you sleep better at night. So I went home and sold my gun and I bought you this. For the last few months you have been complaining how much you want Xbox Live, but that your financial advisor, your wife, won't let you have it. So I bought this for you. So for my life, here, this is yours."

The manager at Microsoft had prayed and prayed to make a difference. He thought his time of waiting for an opportunity was just a waste of time. It wasn't. God was in the details — in the conversations — in the pats on the back — in the little laughs. He thought of quitting his job. He didn't know God was using him to save a life. Patience is resisting the immediate to receive God's best.

Imagine your life lived in complete trust in God, knowing his ways are better than your ways. Imagine the confidence you will have in difficult times knowing God's best will eventually turn up. Imagine the courage you will have living every day knowing God has your back. Just be patient. His best for your life is coming. Amen.

New Year's Day
Matthew 25:31-46

When the Son of Man comes in his glory, and all the angels with him, then he will sit on the throne of his glory. All the nations will be gathered before him, and he will separate people one from another as a shepherd separates the sheep from the goats, and he will put the sheep at his right hand and the goats at the left. Then the king will say to those at his right hand, "Come, you that are blessed by my Father, inherit the kingdom prepared for you from the foundation of the world; for I was hungry and you gave me food, I was thirsty and you gave me something to drink, I was a stranger and you welcomed me, I was naked and you gave me clothing, I was sick and you took care of me, I was in prison and you visited me." Then the righteous will answer him, "Lord, when was it that we saw you hungry and gave you food, or thirsty and gave you something to drink? And when was it that we saw you a stranger and welcomed you, or naked and gave you clothing? And when was it that we saw you sick or in prison and visited you?" And the king will answer them, "Truly I tell you, just as you did it to one of the least of these who are members of my family, you did it to me." Then he will say to those at his left hand, "You that are accursed, depart from me into the eternal fire prepared for the devil and his angels; for I was hungry and you gave me no food, I was thirsty and you gave me nothing to drink, I was a stranger and you did not welcome me, naked and you did not give me clothing, sick and in prison and you did not visit me." Then they also will answer, "Lord, when was it that we saw you hungry or thirsty or a stranger or naked or sick or in prison, and did not take care of you?" Then he will answer them, "Truly I tell you, just as you did not do it to one of the least of these, you did not do it to me." And these will go away into eternal punishment, but the righteous into eternal life.

Addicted to Hurry

As a pastor, I speak with many people who feel that their lives are runaway trains about to slide off the track. They no longer enjoy life and its blessings but live every day with stress, fear, dread, and fatigue. What contributes to living life in this unhealthy way is the misguided belief that faster is better. Rarely is this true. The only thing faster gives us is a sure way to live every day exhausted. Our Lord does not want us to live life this way. He said, "I have come that you might have life in all of its abundance." He didn't say, "I have come that you might experience stress in all of its abundance."

I want to focus on our addiction to hurry and show us how we can slow down, enjoy life, and still get everything done. I remember when I was living in Orlando I went to the store one day to buy a swimsuit for my vacation. We were leaving that very day and I was rushing around. I went to the store and bought the suit. As I was rushing back to my car my cell phone rang. It was my wife. She wanted me to pick up a few more things before we left. As I was talking with her, I put the bag containing the swimsuit on top of the car so I could open the door. I quickly got in, shut the door, and drove away. As I was driving around, people started acting crazy. They were pointing at me and laughing. They were beeping their horns at me. I thought, "What in the world is going on?" I looked to my left and I could see my swimsuit flapping in the wind like a flag. I had left the bag on top of the car at the store and shut the door on the swimsuit! I can only imagine what people were thinking of me as they saw my shorts flying in the wind.

Rushing is never helpful. Hurrying affects us physically, emotionally, and spiritually. We all know this but we continue to hurry anyway. Why? We all believe that it is better to hurry because we think if we hurry we will get more done and if we get more done we are more productive, successful, and important. When people ask us how we are doing we love saying, "I am so busy. There are just not enough hours in the day! I have a thousand things to do today!" What we are saying is "I am more important than you! Look at how successful I am and how needed I am." Somehow the winner is the one who is the busiest and the most miserable. There must be a better way!

I am going to tell you there is a way for you to not hurry and still get everything done that needs to get done. That's right. It's true. There is a way for you to slow down, enjoy life, and still get everything done. Some of you don't know how that is possible because you have been conditioned to believe that busier and faster is better, but this is a fallacy. Leo Babauta reminds us: "Is a book better if you speed read it, or if you take your time and get lost in it? Is a song better if you skim through it, or if you take the time to really listen? Life as a whole is better if you go slowly, take the time to savor it, and appreciate every moment."

Maybe you are thinking that all of this is true but it is not realistic. Perhaps you are thinking, "I wish I had the luxury of slowing down but I have kids to feed, bills to pay, soccer games to attend, and meetings to attend. There are things that need to get done and I have to hurry most of the time. That is just the way it is." What I am saying to you today is that you can slow down and savor the life God has blessed you with and still get everything done. How is that possible? How do we do that? I want us to take a look at some powerful words Jesus said that could make all the difference to your life. These words have the power to get your life back on track and can enable you to live at a pace that allows you to enjoy life and get everything done.

These words come from the gospel of Matthew, chapter 6:

> Therefore I tell you, do not worry about your life, what you will eat or drink; or about your body, what you will wear. Is not life more important than food, and the body more important than clothes? (v. 25 NIV)

Jesus is telling us to get some perspective. The things we worry about and rush to get done are not always the most important things in life.

> Look at the birds of the air; they do not sow or reap or store away in barns, and yet your heavenly Father feeds them. Are you not much more valuable than they? (v. 26 NIV)

This is priceless. This is Jesus getting "Zen" on us. Jesus is telling us to take a look at nature. Do you ever see a bird or any other animal for that matter rushing around and worrying all the time about getting things done? Do you ever see a tree acting frantic? No, and yet everything gets done. Water flows, the sun shines, the grass grows but it never rushes, and it all gets done. We are more important in God's eyes than water or grass so why do we rush and worry?

> Who of you by worrying can add a single hour to his life? (v. 27 NIV)

This was Jesus cracking a joke. Has rushing, hurrying, and worrying extended your life (some translations say, "add to your height")? Has worrying ever made you taller or better? Does hurrying and worrying make your life better? No. It actually makes it worse.

And why do you worry about clothes? See how the lilies of the field grow. They do not labor or spin. Yet I tell you that not even Solomon in all his splendor was dressed like one of these. (vv. 28-29 NIV)

This is Jesus getting Zen on us again. Look at flowers. Do you see flowers laboring, spinning, rushing, worrying, or shaking? No! Yet their needs are taken care of.

If that is how God clothes the grass of the field, which is here today and tomorrow is thrown into the fire, will he not much more clothe you, O you of little faith? (v. 30 NIV)

If that is how God treats flowers and they don't worry why do we as his children rush around and worry?

So do not worry, saying, "What shall we eat?" or "What shall we drink?" or "What shall we wear?" For the pagans run after all these things, and your heavenly Father knows that you need them. (vv. 31-32 NIV)

The people who don't believe and trust in God are always rushing and hurrying around like everything depends on them. We know better.

But seek first his kingdom and his righteousness, and all these things will be given to you as well. (v. 33 NIV)

Concentrate on what is most important and everything will fall into place.

Therefore do not worry about tomorrow, for tomorrow will worry about itself. Each day has enough trouble of its own. (v. 34 NIV)

Jesus is telling to not get ahead of ourselves. What needs to be done tomorrow we can focus on tomorrow. Let's cross that bridge when we get to it. Now, Jesus is not saying there are not things to be concerned about. There are! Jesus is saying there are things that are right in front of us today, at this very moment, that are important and need our attention. Don't miss it! Let's not miss what is important now by rushing to what we think might be important later. Here is something to remember: Moving quickly gets things done but slowing down gets the right things done.

You can move quickly and rush and worry and say, "Look at all that I got done!" But look at what you might have missed in the process. In your rushing you may have missed what was most important and that makes all that you got done meaningless.

You may have felt good about taking that call during your son's baseball game but when he came to bat you were still on the phone and missed the double he hit. You may think you need to go over in your mind all the things that need to get done tomorrow in the car, but you will miss your little girl telling you about the picture she drew in class she is proud of. One day that little girl will grow up and you will wish you had that moment back. You may think that checking your texts at the dinner table with your spouse is just what you do, but later you may wonder why you don't feel as connected and why the intimacy has faded. Those are the moments that count. You may think skipping worship or your devotional time to get more work done around the house will make you feel better but is replacing a light bulb more important than feeding your soul and developing your relationship with Christ?

How do we apply this critical principle in our lives today so that we can start living without hurry and worry and live life with joy and focus? Two simple things:

Some things may need to wait until tomorrow. And that's okay. Some of you may be thinking, "Wait, I thought you said everything will get done." I did say that, but some things that are not as important may need to wait until tomorrow or next week. There's always tomorrow. The world will not end if you don't get that task done today. What needs to get done will get done.

Simplify your life. When you focus on the most important things in life without hurrying, your life begins to prioritize almost by itself. Take a look at what has been pushed aside and be honest about whether those things are necessary. Maybe some things are not necessary anymore. Perhaps it is time to simplify your life.

A beautiful thing happens when we stop rushing and hurrying — the important things emerge and the unnecessary things fade into the background. I think that is one of the things Jesus had in mind when he told us that if we get our priorities straight we will be doing the things that matter to him like serving others and bringing hope to the hopeless. Jesus said if we concentrate on that it is just like we are serving him (Matthew 25:40 NIV).

A profound example of this occurred in Buffalo, New York, a while back when a school bus driver lived out the principle that slowing down gets the right things done.

On October 18, 2013, 37-year-old Darnell Barton was driving a bus full of high school students on an expressway overpass when he spotted a woman on the wrong side of the guard rail. She looked like she was about to take her own life. He said, "It didn't seem real because of what was going on around; traffic and pedestrians were going by as normal." Several bikers and runners rushed passed her and never noticed what was going on right in front of them.

A surveillance camera showed Barton stopping his bus next to the woman. She was distraught and in her own world. Barton repeatedly asked if she was okay and she never responded. Barton then carefully walked up to the woman so he could pull her to safety. "She turned back to look at me and then back at the traffic and that's when I kind of lunged and got my left arm around her body," Barton told the Buffalo News. "I asked her, 'Do you want to come on this side of the guardrail now?' and that was the first time she spoke to me and said, 'Yeah.' "

Barton sat with her until the police and firefighters arrived. Later, he got back on the bus and finished his shift. The kids on the bus applauded and later each of them shook his hand as they got off the bus (source: Huffingtonpost.com).

How did Darnell see her and others didn't? Darnell was going at a pace which allowed him to see what was most important. Was he late finishing his shift? Yeah. Did he probably save a woman's life? Oh yes. Moving quickly gets things done but slowing down gets the right things done. Amen.

Christmas 2
John 1:(1-9) 10-18

In the beginning was the Word, and the Word was with God, and the Word was God. He was in the beginning with God. All things came into being through him, and without him not one thing came into being. What has come into being in him was life, and the life was the light of all people. The light shines in the darkness, and the darkness did not overcome it. There was a man sent from God, whose name was John. He came as a witness to testify to the light, so that all might believe through him. He himself was not the light, but he came to testify to the light. The true light, which enlightens everyone, was coming into the world. He was in the world, and the world came into being through him; yet the world did not know him. He came to what was his own, and his own people did not accept him. But to all who received him, who believed in his name, he gave power to become children of God, who were born, not of blood or of the will of the flesh or of the will of man, but of God. And the Word became flesh and lived among us, and we have seen his glory, the glory as of a father's only son, full of grace and truth. (John testified to him and cried out, "This was he of whom I said, 'He who comes after me ranks ahead of me because he was before me.' ") From his fullness we have all received, grace upon grace. The law indeed was given through Moses; grace and truth came through Jesus Christ. No one has ever seen God. It is God the only Son, who is close to the Father's heart, who has made him known.

Less Is More

I want to share with you a simple biblical message about how to find contentment. So often our lives get out of control because we fall under the spell of a terrible myth. The myth is that more is better — the more we have, achieve, attain, or buy the happier we will be. This myth is no more powerful than during the Christmas season which has just come and gone. We saw all the ads promising utopia if we bought the perfect Christmas present. Many of us bought those presents and still no utopia. How long did it take those toys to break or lose their luster? Not long.

Many of us have played the "if only game" — "If only I had a new car, then I would be happy... If only I got a better job, then I would be happy... If only we could be in a bigger house, then we would be happy." Maybe you got some of these things and you experienced pleasure for a little while, but guess what happened? When the newness wore off — when the novelty wore off — when the cool factor wore off the feelings of being unsatisfied returned. Then it was on to another goal or desire.

We spend so much of our lives thinking that happiness is on the other side of some future event. We think that once we get there we will be happy. You have probably felt that way your whole life and you are still not happy. When you were a kid you thought that when you grew up and left home you would be happy. Then you thought once you got married you would be happy. Then you thought when you had children you would be happy and satisfied. Then many of you thought or think that once you get your children out of the house you will be happy!

Some of us think we will be happy once we get through some difficulty or problem. We really believe that once we survive this hardship or jump over this hurdle or get through this difficulty then life will be just like we want it. So we fight, survive, jump, and push through. And then what do we find? Another challenge staring us in the face! That's life.

We all want to be happy and content. David Veerman writes, "Many of us make happiness a lifelong pursuit as we spend money, collect things, and search for new and better experiences. But what happens when the toys rust, loved ones die, health deteriorates, money is stolen, and the party is over?" What happens when despair sets in once again and there is still a vacuum in our lives and we are still not content with our lives?

It is clear that learning to simplify our lives is the answer. Try to get along in life with less. The richest people are those with the fewest needs. Clear the clutter out and don't rely on so much to make you happy. Simplify, simplify; less is more. It sounds easy. Take stock and get rid of what you don't really need that is complicating your life. It is simple. But why don't more people do it? Because living with less to get more and simplifying your life starts from the inside out. You could go out today and sell half of your possessions and try to live on less but unless your heart is truly changed you will go right back to trying to accumulate more and never be content.

So how do we go about changing our heart to find contentment and learning that less is more? Let me share with you an experience I had with a friend of mine a few years ago. He came to visit me. He had lost a lot of weight, and he looked much different. It all started several months back when he became very depressed. He was struggling with his job. His wife was threatening to leave him. He had mounting debt. They were about to foreclose on his house. To make matters worse, he developed a rare disease that left him almost paralyzed and he was forced into the hospital for several days. While he was in the hospital, he did a lot of thinking and praying and he discovered God again. He also became aware of all the friends he had in his life.

Fortunately, my friend recovered and he came to see me in my office. I prayed with him and, as I prayed, he squeezed my hand so tight I thought he was going to squeeze it off. When I finished praying, there were tears in his eyes. He looked up at me and said, "I've found the way to peace in my life. I don't know why it took me so long to learn it. I've learned to be grateful, not angry." He was right.

The way to contentment is through an attitude of gratitude. An attitude of gratitude is appreciating the good things in your life and giving thanks to God for all his blessings. John 1:16 (NIV) plainly tells us, "From the fullness of his grace we have all received one blessing after another." How true. But how often do we stop and think about all of our blessings and thank God for them? The Bible tells us to do this over and over again. Look at Paul's words in Colossians 3:15-17:

> And let the peace of Christ rule in your hearts, to which indeed you were called in the one body. And be thankful. Let the word of Christ dwell in you richly; teach and admonish one another in all wisdom; and with gratitude in your hearts sing psalms, hymns, and spiritual songs to God. And whatever you do, in word or deed, do everything in the name of the Lord Jesus, giving thanks to God the Father through him.

The more we appreciate the good in our life the more good appreciates and overshadows the bad things in our life. An attitude of gratitude is like a magnet that pulls in the power and guidance of God into our lives. What's more is that an attitude of gratitude gives us a better disposition, more joy, more energy, and is just plain healthy. There have been medical studies that have proven the healing power of gratitude.

Where do we begin? Well, if you begin cultivating gratitude in three things you can't go wrong. If you begin with these things you are guaranteed to be happy and content with your life.

First, you will never find happiness and joy until you appreciate yourself and are grateful for who God made you to be.

Back in the 80s there was a popular song sung by Whitney Houston titled "The Greatest Love Of All." It is a beautiful song. It tells that the greatest love is easy to achieve. It is learning to love yourself. Why is this the greatest love of all? Learning to love yourself is learning to see yourself the way God sees you.

Saint Bernard lived hundreds of years ago. He was a very wise man. He took all of the lessons he had learned about faith and life and summed them up through what he called the four stages of spiritual growth. You may find them surprising.

• Love of self for self's sake
• Love of God for self's sake
• Love of God for God's sake
• Love of self for God's sake

Isn't that amazing? The final stage of spiritual growth is loving yourself the way God loves you!

I remember a young lady in a church I served. She was active in the youth group and was president of everything in school. She had wonderful grades and everyone was so proud of her. She got into the college of her choice and I kept up with her by email. I will never forget an email she sent me that read, "Pastor Charley, I've just made the most important decision of my life." She went on to tell me what happened. She and her friends were invited to a fraternity party off campus. They were not sure about going, but there was going to be a guy at the party that she really liked so they decided to go.

They drove to the party. It was on a farm and there was a big bonfire with lots of beer. She saw the guy she liked; he came up to her and started to talk to her. She was so excited. After a few minutes, he opened up his hand and there were a few marijuana joints. He said to her, "Why don't you come off with me and we will smoke these?" She wrote, "I really wanted to do it because I liked this guy, but I knew it was wrong. Then," she wrote, "suddenly I felt a presence come over me. It felt like there was someone above me. I knew it was Jesus. He said, 'Don't do that. You're worth more than that.' " She then wrote, "I didn't do it. God loves me too much and I love myself too much to do that." And she left the party early. She concluded the email by saying, "I've never been happier. I'm so proud of my decision."

Happiness is found in knowing your worth and being grateful for who you are. Happiness is found in making choices out of the knowledge that you matter to God. Someone once said that "the greatest thing that can happen is to be able to look yourself in the mirror and like what you see."

Second, to find contentment, it is important to appreciate the people in your life. Life is so precious, so it is important to be grateful for people. Human beings are strange creatures. So often we hurt the ones closest to us.

A colleague tells of going to his doctor for a check-up. He and his doctor were friends. After the examination was over, the doctor took off his stethoscope and said, "Now, will you examine me? I've got to get something off my chest that is bothering me." My colleague said, "Sure. What is on your mind?" He went on to talk about his only daughter who just went through a bitter divorce. He said that they had so much promise when they first got married, but he mentioned that the last two years they were married he never heard them compliment each other. He always heard them talk about one another's faults. He said to my colleague, "I think it could have made a difference. If they could have looked for something to appreciate about each other, they might still be married and happy."

There is much truth in what that troubled doctor had to say. Appreciating the people in your life can heal deep wounds. Choosing to see the good in others can keep love alive. Recent research has shown that healthy married couples say something affirming to one another five times a day.

I've learned that criticism does not do any good. Our culture puts a high value on criticism but all that does is make things worse. Let's face it. How do you feel when someone comes up to you and asks, "Can I give you some constructive criticism?" None of us look forward to those conversations and we usually leave those conversations feeling bad about ourselves. Criticism does not do any good. But honest appreciation works like magic. In fact, honest appreciation can change lives. So after you finish reading this chapter think of someone you appreciate, call them, and tell them why you appreciate them. You never know what a difference it will make.

Several years ago in Detroit there was a little boy by the name of Stevie Morris. He found himself in a classroom one day. A little mouse got loose in the classroom and all the kids jumped on their desks and started to scream. The teacher asked Stevie to help her find the mouse, since he had such remarkable ears. He had exceptional hearing because he was blind. It was the first time anyone had shown appreciation for Stevie. The teacher had no idea the ripple effect of that appreciation. Stevie went on to develop his hearing and became pretty well known. Maybe you have heard of him — Stevie Wonder?

Who do you appreciate? Give thanks for them and tell them thanks. You never know what a difference it will make.

Finally the one person in the Bible who can teach us a great deal about finding contentment is Paul. In fact, he actually said that he had learned the secret of being content. Have you ever heard anyone say that? Well, as Paul was on death row awaiting execution he would write about it in Philippians 4:11-13:

> For I have learned to be content with whatever I have. I know what it is to have little, and I know what it is to have plenty. In any and all circumstances I have learned the secret of being well-fed and of going hungry, of having plenty and of being in need. I can do all things through him who strengthens me.

Paul's secret had nothing to do with him, what he knew, what he accomplished, the trouble he avoided, or the success he may have attained. Paul's happiness was found in his relationship with God in Jesus Christ. It was the depth of his relationship with God that gave him strength and contentment. Paul was wise enough to know that if you rely on circumstances to make you happy, you will always be disappointed because circumstances always change. But if you rely on the presence of God in your life to make you happy it doesn't matter what you are faced with. You can always be happy because God never changes. God will always love you and he will never let you go.

Someone once put it this way: "Happiness depends on happenings, but joy depends on Christ." Contentment and joy is not about what is "out there" or "down the road," or on the other side of an obstacle or achievement. Contentment is about the God who lives within you. It is about the present moment with God who is always faithful in guiding you and supporting you. When you rely on God and make him the center of your life, you will always have joy no matter where you are in your life.

Norman Vincent Peale remembers going to hear a famous intellectual speak at First Baptist Church of Syracuse, New York. The speaker said something that shocked Peale. He said, "I've never been discouraged the last 25 years of my life!" Peale said that he could not dismiss him as a crank or a nut because he was this famous intellectual. In fact, he was a patron saint of Methodism. His name was E. Stanley Jones. He was a missionary to India, and his job was to convert the intellectuals of India to Christ. He was brilliant.

That night Jones went on to say that the reason he had never been discouraged is that he had discovered a simple workable secret. He said he was trying to carry everything himself, which is why he had two nervous breakdowns. One night while praying in a church service he felt Jesus say to him, "Look Stanley, are you ready to turn your life over to me? Just give it to me and I will give you peace, health, energy, and a great life." Jones said he did it right then and he was never the same.

Are you desperate for contentment and peace? Put your life in Jesus' hands. If your life is out of control, all you need to do is give your life to Jesus. Ask him to come into your heart and forgive your sins and put a new and right spirit within you. Then live your life in obedience to him. This is the only way to find true peace. As the old bumper sticker says: "No Jesus? No peace? Know Jesus. Know Peace."

Perhaps you have already given your life to Christ but you have drifted away. It is time to come back home. It is time to rededicate your life to Christ and find the peace you used to know. It is time. Amen.

Epiphany of Our Lord
Matthew 2:1-12

In the time of King Herod, after Jesus was born in Bethlehem of Judea, wise men from the East came to Jerusalem, asking, "Where is the child who has been born king of the Jews? For we observed his star at its rising, and have come to pay him homage." When King Herod heard this, he was frightened, and all Jerusalem with him; and calling together all the chief priests and scribes of the people, he inquired of them where the Messiah was to be born. They told him, "In Bethlehem of Judea; for so it has been written by the prophet: 'And you, Bethlehem, in the land of Judah, are by no means least among the rulers of Judah; for from you shall come a ruler who is to shepherd my people Israel.' " Then Herod secretly called for the wise men and learned from them the exact time when the star had appeared. Then he sent them to Bethlehem, saying, "Go and search diligently for the child; and when you have found him, bring me word so that I may also go and pay him homage." When they had heard the king, they set out; and there, ahead of them, went the star that they had seen at its rising, until it stopped over the place where the child was. When they saw that the star had stopped, they were overwhelmed with joy. On entering the house, they saw the child with Mary his mother; and they knelt down and paid him homage. Then, opening their treasure chests, they offered him gifts of gold, frankincense, and myrrh. And having been warned in a dream not to return to Herod, they left for their own country by another road.

The Power of Appreciation

I heard a story about twin boys who were polar opposites. One was the eternal pessimist. He saw the negative in everything. The glass was always half empty. The other one was the eternal optimist. He always saw the sunny side to things. He always saw the glass half full.

The twins' parents were curious about this so they took their twin boys to a therapist. The therapist was also curious about how different they were so he put the pessimist in a room full of toys and observed him. The boy picked up a plane and said, "This one is awful. I've seen other planes a lot better than this ugly one." Then he picked up a Matchbox® car and said, "This one is terrible. My friend has a better matchbox car than this one." He did that with every toy.

Then the therapist put the optimist in a room full of manure and the boy immediately started digging. The therapist asked, "What are you doing? Why are you digging?" The boy replied, "Well, with all this manure, there's got to be a horse in here somewhere!" That's optimism! Attitude is everything. It's all in how you look at things.

It is my belief that most of us need an attitude adjustment about Christmas. Yes, Christmas. Perhaps you are thinking, "Wait a second. Christmas is over." Is it? I want to suggest to you that Christmas is not over on December 26. Christmas is just the beginning. The true meaning of Christmas is not something you need just for one day. You don't wrap up Christmas and store it away for next year. What we find at Christmas is something we need every day. This is what the season of Epiphany is all about.

The story about the Magi in Matthew reminds us that what we find at Christmas is life-changing and sustains us every day of our lives. The Magi traveled a long way to worship the Christ Child. They had followed that beautiful star in the east and it led them to the humble place where Jesus was born. When they saw the Christ they were overcome with joy. They opened their treasures and presented him with extravagant gifts.

What was it about Jesus that caused the Magi to travel so far and give so extravagantly? What was it about Jesus that gave them such irreplaceable joy? To better understand what the Magi found in Jesus, let me tell you an old legend about God and Jesus. On the night of Christmas, Jesus was getting ready to go to earth. Just before he left heaven that night Jesus asked, "Any advice, Father? What do you want me to tell them?" God replied, "Don't complicate things. Just tell them how much I love them."

For thousands of years scholars and theologians have filled libraries telling us who they think God is. But you can take all that the theologians have written about God and it would not come close to how the Bible is able to explain God in three simple words — "God is love" (1 John 4:16). God is in love with you. You were made from God's love. That is what God wants us to receive and experience at Christmas. I believe the Magi experienced this love when they saw Christ and it is what caused them to be overjoyed.

This is why I like this text in Matthew to appear after Christmas. Just in case the busyness of the season caused us to miss the true love of Christmas, we can read about the Magi and experience God's love at this very moment. We don't have to wait for next Christmas.

What does this love from God look and feel like? What does it mean for your life? What do we find when we experience God's love at Christmas? We find a self we can live with.

There is a great story about the actor Kirk Douglas. He picked up a hitchhiker on a California freeway one day. The hitchhiker took off his coat and settled down for the ride when suddenly he realized who was driving. He couldn't believe Kirk Douglas had picked him up! Excited and overwhelmed, the hitchhiker asked, "Do you know who you are?"

I want to ask you: Do you know who you are? Some people think they are what they do. We are doctors, lawyers, businessmen, homemakers, plumbers, and mechanics. We do invest ourselves in what we do, don't we? But who are we when we retire or lose our jobs?

Some would have us believe that we are what we have, what we own. We are what is in our bank account. We are the car we drive. But what happens when the toys rust and the money is gone? Does having nothing mean *we* are nothing?

Let me tell you who you are. You are a child of God. You were created in the image of God. You were loved into existence by God who loves you more than you could ever imagine. Jesus said it well, "Anyone who loves me I will come to him and make my home in him." You are loved by God and when you accept and experience that love, you discover that you were not created by accident. God took time to form you and shape you. You are special.

In Christ we also find a God we can count on. I have discovered that many people are turned off by faith, church, and religion because, quite frankly, people make it too complicated. The Christian faith was never meant to be complicated.

I am going tell you what the faith is all about and make it as uncomplicated as I can. What I am going to tell you sums up my theological education. In fact, if you receive what I am about to tell you, you will have the equivalent of a doctoral degree in Christian theology. Here goes. Christianity is not a religion, creed, a liturgy, or a set of prayers. Christianity is not a bunch of rules and regulations or a good moral story. Christianity is a *relationship* — a relationship with the one who loved you into existence — a relationship with one who thinks you are beautiful — a relationship with the one who has a purpose for your life and loves you more than you can imagine — a relationship with a God you can count on. God could have chosen to reveal himself to us in an easier way but because he wants a relationship with us, God became one of us in Christ. He came to show us that he loves us and we can count on him no matter what.

You see, Christians are not perfect. Christians are not in control. Christians don't have all the answers. Christians are not better than other people. Christians are not folks who can give the perfect theological answer to every question. Christians are those who have learned that God can be trusted. God can be trusted to give peace in the midst of the storm. God can be trusted to take what is evil and transform it into something good. God can be trusted to empower you in the midst of trouble. God can be trusted to receive you when you die. God can be trusted!

The late great spiritual writer Henri Nouwen received the greatest revelation about faith at the circus! Nouwen went to see the German trapeze group "The Flying Rodleighs" perform. He was mesmerized by their breathtaking performance as they flew gracefully through the air. At the end of the show, he spoke with the leader of the troupe, Rodleigh himself. Nouwen asked him how he was able to perform with such grace and ease so high in the air. Rodleigh responded, "The public might think that I am the great star of the trapeze, but the real star is Joe, my catcher... The secret is that the flyer does nothing and the catcher does everything. When I fly to Joe, I have simply to stretch out my arms and hands and wait for him to catch me. The worst thing the flyer can do is try to catch the catcher. I'm not supposed to catch Joe. It's Joe's task to catch me."[1]

So often we try to grab onto God. We think that if we read enough books and go to enough Bible studies, we can catch God. We think if we do enough mental gymnastics or enough fanciful praying, we can catch God. It's not our job to catch God. God catches us. This is what Christmas is all about. God catches our hearts through Jesus Christ.

In Christ we also find a love worth sharing. First John 4:11-12 says, "Beloved, since God loves us so much, we also ought to love one another. No one has ever seen God; if we love one another, God lives in us, and his love is perfected in us."

I have found that so many people want to experience God in their lives. And many people will pay large sums of money to go to exotic places to experience God. They will go to conferences and retreats to experience God. There is nothing wrong with any of these things, but there is a simple way to experience God that will not cost us anything. Do you want to experience God today? Give away God's love. His love is perfected within us when we share his love with world! Believe me, you will feel God when you share his love with others.

Someone once said, "You haven't lived until you have loved, and if you haven't loved, you haven't lived." There are people everywhere who are hungry for God's love. There are people we come across every day who are hungry for someone to tell them that they are loved.

Peter Breemen wrote the book *The God Who Won't Let Go*. In the book he tells of the time he was in a grocery store late at night with only one checkout line open. There was a long line of restless and impatient people waiting with their groceries. Breemen noticed that the people in front of the line were in a good mood. As he got closer to the checkout, he figured out why. The lady checking groceries took a piece of cardboard, made a sign, and put it in front of her. The sign said, "We have been made with love, please treat us accordingly."

Peter Breemen defines love in a very special way: "Love is revealing to someone else that person's own beauty."

Loving is showing someone else how beautiful he or she is. A person cannot discover this alone, another human being is needed. When one human being shows another human being how beautiful they are, then love happens. That's what God in Jesus does for us — he shows us how beautiful we are. This experience compels us to show others how beautiful they are to God.

USA Today recently reported a story that embodies this definition of love. It happened in North Carolina at a Pizza Hut. A single mom took her four-year-old daughter and six-year-old son out for pizza. That doesn't seem like a big deal, but it can be a very big deal when your son has Aspergers and ADHD and your daughter has her own behavioral problems.

After they arrived, she apologized in advance to a man sitting nearby because her kids tended to be loud and obnoxious. She even suggested that he might want to move to the other side of the restaurant. The man said he didn't mind and he went about eating his meal. For the next several minutes the mom did her best to control her kids in a public environment.

When the man left the restaurant, the waitress approached the woman's table and informed her that the man who was sitting beside them had paid her bill, left a gift card, and written her a three-page letter. Part of the letter read, "I do not know your back story, but I have had the privilege of watching you parent your children for the past thirty minutes. I have watched you teach your children about the importance of respect, education, proper manners, communication, self-control, and kindness all while being very patient. I will never cross your path again but am positive that you and your children have amazing futures."

The man did not have to do that but he had a love worth sharing. He showed that mother her own beauty.

Finally in Christ, we find a church we can connect with. One of my favorite Christmas movies is *Home Alone*. You may remember that in the movie Kevin accidentally gets left behind when his family leaves for a European vacation. At first he is thrilled. He has the whole house to himself and all this freedom. Soon, however, he begins to miss his family and becomes very lonely. On Christmas Eve, Kevin stumbles in to a church. He sits in a pew next to an older man who is also unhappy because of family problems. As they engage in conversation, young Kevin confesses that he has not always been the best brother, but he really misses his family. "Well," says the older man, "you're in church now… and this is the place to come when you're feeling bad about yourself."

That man was right. It is because of Christ that we have the church and church is the place to go when we need comfort — when we need forgiveness — when we need to make a new start — when we need peace for our troubled souls. Why? Because Christ dwells with those who love him and church is filled with those who love Christ and love each other. Sometimes we forget how special we are and how much God loves us. This is why we have the church. The church reminds us how beautiful we are to God.

The church is not perfect but the church worships the perfect person who loves us perfectly and that love empowers us to be who God created us to be. That's the message of Christmas and it is a message we desperately need not just one day but every day of the year. Amen.

---

1. Henri J.M. Nouwen, *The Only Necessary Thing: Living a Prayerful Life* (New York: Crossroad Publishing Company, 1999) pp. 195-96.

Baptism of Our Lord
Mark 1:4-11

John the baptizer appeared in the wilderness, proclaiming a baptism of repentance for the forgiveness of sins. And people from the whole Judean countryside and all the people of Jerusalem were going out to him, and were baptized by him in the river Jordan, confessing their sins. Now John was clothed with camel's hair, with a leather belt around his waist, and he ate locusts and wild honey. He proclaimed, "The one who is more powerful than I is coming after me; I am not worthy to stoop down and untie the thong of his sandals. I have baptized you with water; but he will baptize you with the Holy Spirit." In those days Jesus came from Nazareth of Galilee and was baptized by John in the Jordan. And just as he was coming up out of the water, he saw the heavens torn apart and the Spirit descending like a dove on him. And a voice came from heaven, "You are my Son, the Beloved; with you I am well pleased."

The Wind

John the Baptist says something interesting in Mark, "He (Jesus) will baptize you with the Holy Spirit." Those were prophetic words. John was pointing to a time when those who followed Jesus would be infused with the power of the Holy Spirit. Later this prophetic word would be underscored by Jesus' baptism when the Spirit of God descended upon him like a dove. Just a few years later John's words would be confirmed on the day of Pentecost when the church was born by the power of the Holy Spirit. On this historic day God's power exploded through the church and began its mission of making disciples.

It was a day the disciples would never forget. Thousands of people were in Jerusalem celebrating the day that God gave Moses the Ten Commandments. Disciples were gathered together in a house. Suddenly it happened: wind and fire swept through the disciples. Everybody was amazed and astonished. Many thought a drunken party was taking place even though it was only 9 a.m. A huge crowd gathered around Peter as he preached and said, "God has given us the Holy Spirit!" Three thousand people confessed Christ and were baptized.

Pentecost should be the third great holiday of the church, next to Christmas and Easter, but most churches treat it as just another Sunday. This says a lot about the attitude of the modern church regarding the Holy Spirit. Yet, the words of John continue to echo today, "He will baptize you with the Holy Spirit." They remind us that the church was born on the day of Pentecost when the Holy Spirit infused it with the power to change to world.

I remember being invited to a birthday party. It was for one of the children in the church I served. They had the party at home and invited a bunch of children over. It was quite a scene. They had a big blow-up jumpy contraption in the front yard. They hired a clown to make funny balloons. The place was saturated with decorations and banners. There was cake, presents, and games. Most of all, there were excited boys and girls running all over the place.

I was sitting in the living room watching all of the excitement. I was smiling and remembering the excitement of my birthday parties when I was a kid. As I sat there eating cake, I struck up a conversation with an older man sitting next to me. He was the birthday boy's uncle. He didn't look too excited to be there. He said something about it being too noisy and the children being too exuberant. Then he looked at me and said, "It's funny. When you are young you get excited about your birthday, about life and all that is ahead of you. But as you get older, there seems to be less to get excited about. When your birthday comes you are reminded how old you are. People keep saying 'Happy Birthday' to you but there's really nothing happy about it."

I thought about the conversation with that man and came to the conclusion that it is a living parable for how the modern church views Pentecost and the whole idea of the Holy Spirit. Too many of us sit back and observe the story of Pentecost like a noisy party from the past. We understand it. We know it is a part of our history. But we would just as soon eat our cake then go home and take a nap. There may have been a time for all that enthusiasm, wind, and fire, but we are civilized Christians now and we are careful not to get carried away. Some cynic has said that if it were up to most Christians, churches would have lightning rods on their steeples instead of crosses in memory of that time when lightning struck the early church and as protection against it ever happening again.

The truth of this was seen on an ABC News Special titled "In the Name of God." Peter Jennings interviewed the founder of the Vineyard Christian Fellowship, John Wimber. Wimber said that the first time he went to church he expected dramatic things to happen. He had read some of the stories in the Bible and couldn't wait to experience church. After attending three Sundays, he was disappointed and frustrated. Following the service, he talked to an usher and asked him, "When do they do it?" "Do what?" asked the man. "The stuff," Wimber answered. "What stuff?" "The stuff in the Bible." "What do you mean?" "You know, multiplying loaves and fish, feeding the hungry, healing the sick, giving sight to the blind. That stuff." "Oh," the man replied apologetically, "We don't do that. We believe in it, and we pray about it. But we don't do it."

This is true in most churches, especially the mainline church. Many Christians want just enough religion to be comfortable, to be respected, to feel good about themselves, but not so much that it shakes up their routines and changes their way of living. Many Christians want the benefits of the Holy Spirit without having to experience much of the Spirit. Many Christians want to go to the dance without having to dance. Many of us read about Pentecost and the power of the Holy Spirit, smile, and then put it back on the bookshelf next to our favorite novels and DVDs then go back to our lives as usual. Such exuberance is kid stuff, the stuff of movies and myth. After all, you have to be careful with this kind of exuberance. If there is one thing that most modern, mainline Christians are, it is careful.

You can't really blame us for being careful. There's lots of weird stuff that goes on in churches that aren't as careful. I recall being invited by a friend of mine to go to his church. I was in high school. They met in this warehouse.

We sat down and the service began. It seemed like a normal service. There was a worship leader who led praise and worship. People were singing and enjoying worship. Then the preacher got up, and he was rather exuberant. Then he became more exuberant and started to speak in tongues. It sounded like gibberish. The lady next to me started to speak in tongues. People around me started to work themselves into a frenzy. Soon the whole row in front of me was on the floor shaking and writhing. I wanted to call an ambulance for them but then my friend informed me that they were fine. They were "slain in the Spirit!" I said, "Slain in the what?" He said, "The Spirit." I said, "Well, I've got the Spirit too, but it never wanted to hurt me."

I was terrified and told my friend I needed to go to the bathroom. Really I just waited outside until the service was over. The next day I brought my Bible to school and showed my friend where it says in scripture that if you speak in tongues in church there must be a translator. Otherwise it is just showing off. I quickly told him that there are many gifts of the Spirit and speaking in tongues is down on the list. We really do have to be careful with this Holy Spirit business.

I remember sitting in a board meeting at another church. A youth had come to the meeting to propose a plan for evangelism for the church. He had gone to some conference on evangelism. He heard a dynamic speaker, brought some literature, and was excited to get the church to evangelize in the community. When he was called on to speak, he said that if a handful of members went door-to-door in the community they could reach a certain percentage of people for Christ. The chairman of the board quickly told the youth that they were not that kind of church — "We don't go door-to-door bothering people." He said, "Son, we have to be careful about how we present ourselves to the community." We really do have to be careful with this Holy Spirit business.

A colleague of mine was assigned to a new church. He was just out of seminary feeling excited about what God was calling him to do at his first church. It was an older church but they had lots of young people moving into the area. My friend felt led to reach those young people and grow the church. He decided to start a contemporary service. He got a team of people together and made plans. Members of the church who were musicians volunteered to play. A bunch of media equipment was donated. They set a start date and began publicizing it around the community. About a week before the very first service my friend found the donated drums, speakers, and guitars piled up outside his office. On top of the pile was a note from concerned members of the church. It said, "Dear Pastor: If you continue with this new-fangled service, we will write the bishop and tell him you are incompetent and not fit to serve our church." He continued with the service but a year later, he was voted out of the church. We have to be careful with all this Holy Spirit business, don't we?

He didn't like what his church was doing. He felt it didn't have much life. It wasn't doing the things that a church ought to be doing. It wasn't praying enough and serving enough. It wasn't studying the Bible enough. So, he, led by the Spirit, started all of these small groups in the church. Lo and behold, they started to catch on, got all fired up, started to change things, and shake things up. The leader of this crew started to speak all across town. He lifted up the gospel and all of these people listened to him and responded. They received Christ. He was the talk of the town. His church was none too pleased with all this excitement and exuberance, with all this change. They got annoyed with this group in the church and their leader. What did the church do? They wouldn't allow him to speak in church anymore. His name was John Wesley. The group was the Methodists! We have to be careful with all of this Holy Spirit business, don't we?

We have become really good at being careful of the Spirit over the years. We have become really good at putting a governor on the Spirit of God. We have become rather skilled at stifling the Spirit when it doesn't line up with our whims and fancies or it threatens to inconvenience us. The Spirit is strong but it doesn't force itself on anyone or any church, so it will go only as far as we allow it.

Thank goodness, right? Because it's much easier running the church on our own, without being bothered by the Spirit, isn't it? A church can survive while keeping the Spirit at bay. It just needs to be organized, be nice, be civilized, and be careful. All it has to do is find a good speaker to tell nice stories, find a good band to play good music, and the church will be well on its way with being pleased with itself. Sure, there is only so much you can accomplish without the aid of the Spirit, but at least you look good. At least you are in control.

For 132 years America's Cup was kept and defended by the United States, but in 1983 Australia threatened to take the cup away from America. They were tied with three wins each. On the day of the final race, the whole world was watching. Australia was going crazy. Scores of people came to watch the race and television crews we ready to broadcast it all over the world. All was ready but there was no race. Why? There was no wind. Experienced racer Allan Walker said of that day, "In yachting, no wind means no race."

It's true. Nothing happens without the wind. In the Bible the Hebrew and Greek word for "Spirit" literally means "wind." The great preacher Fred Craddock says, "I cannot describe the Holy Spirit. I cannot explain the Spirit of God. Jesus said it is like a mystery, like the wind. You don't see the wind, yet you know when it comes and when it goes."

Craddock remembers seeing a big wall standing proud. It didn't need anybody or anything. He passed it another day and it had crumbled to the ground. He wondered what caused it. Someone told him it was the wind. The wall reminded Craddock of a man he once knew who was hardened by life. He hated the church. He didn't need help from anyone or anything. Then one day all that bitterness crumbled to the ground. His heart was changed. Craddock wondered what caused the man to change and someone suggested to him it was the wind.

I understand the mysterious power of the wind. My wife and I were staying with some friends. I woke up in the middle of the night to the sound of chimes outside the window. I said, "What is that?" My wife answered, "Well, it's the wind!"

I heard about a church that was about to close its doors. It was old and tired. One day all these people starting coming to the church. It started to grow. I asked, "What happened?" Someone said, "It's the wind."

There I was sixteen years old, minding my own business. I was playing tennis, getting crushes on girls, telling jokes, and having fun. I was sitting in church with my parents. We were passing the mints, playing tic-tac-toe, and writing notes about where we wanted to go to lunch. Then this man got up to preach. I was inspired. Next thing I know I am shaking the minister's hand at the door telling him I want to be a preacher! Me, a preacher? What happened? What caused that? You know what I think it was? The wind. Amen.

Epiphany 2
Ordinary Time 2
John 1:43-51

The next day Jesus decided to go to Galilee. He found Philip and said to him, "Follow me." Now Philip was from Bethsaida, the city of Andrew and Peter. Philip found Nathanael and said to him, "We have found him about whom Moses in the law and also the prophets wrote, Jesus son of Joseph from Nazareth." Nathanael said to him, "Can anything good come out of Nazareth?" Philip said to him, "Come and see." When Jesus saw Nathanael coming toward him, he said of him, "Here is truly an Israelite in whom there is no deceit!" Nathanael asked him, "Where did you get to know me?" Jesus answered, "I saw you under the fig tree before Philip called you." Nathanael replied, "Rabbi, you are the Son of God! You are the King of Israel!" Jesus answered, "Do you believe because I told you that I saw you under the fig tree? You will see greater things than these." And he said to him, "Very truly, I tell you, you will see heaven opened and the angels of God ascending and descending upon the Son of Man."

Mission Possible!

Jesus and Moses went golfing one day. Jesus was about to hit a shot and said, "Hey Moses, watch this! Just like Arnold Palmer!" Moses said, "Jesus, you can do anything but don't try to be like Arnold Palmer." Jesus said, "No, watch this — just like Arnold Palmer!"

Jesus hit the ball in the water so Jesus asked Moses to get the ball. Moses parted the water and got the ball. This continued for about fifteen minutes. Finally, Jesus hit the ball in the water for the seventh time. "Please get my ball for me," Jesus asked Moses. Moses said, "No, I told you to quit trying to be like Arnold Palmer so I'm not getting it this time."

Jesus walked across the water, reached down, and got his ball. While he was doing this, a couple rode by in a cart and said, "Who does he think he is, Jesus?" Moses said, "No! He thinks he's Arnold Palmer!"

All of us can't be like Arnold Palmer, but all of us can be like Jesus! In fact, we have been called to be like Jesus — to love like Jesus — to make a difference like Jesus — to change the world like Jesus. The Bible says we have been empowered to be like Jesus.

I think this is what compelled Philip and the rest of the disciples to drop everything and follow him. Jesus simply said to Philip, "Follow me" and he did, right on the spot (John 1:43). There was a great call of adventure and meaning in those two simple words of Jesus. Philip and the disciples couldn't resist.

Jesus' irresistible call is also seen later in the gospel of John: "You will do greater works than me because I am going to the Father" (John 14:12 paraphrased). How is it possible that we can do greater works than Jesus? Jesus has always been. In the first chapter of John we read, "In the beginning was the Word, and the Word was with God, and the Word was God." But when Jesus was on earth in human form his influence was limited. He could only heal one person at a time and teach to groups at a time but when Jesus went back to the Father, his Holy Spirit came to live in each of his followers. In this way, Jesus' influence is multiplied through us and we can reach the whole world together! This is what Jesus means by doing greater works than him. We have been given power through the Holy Spirit to be like Jesus in this world. This is why our mission to make disciples is possible!

Jesus not only spoke about the power to be like him in John. It is also mentioned in the synoptic gospels — Matthew, Mark, and Luke. We give a lot of credence to his last words. We believe what people say is important before they leave the earth. Have you ever paid attention to Jesus' last words to his disciples before he left the earth? In Matthew 28:16-20 Jesus' last words to his disciples were "Go and make disciples..." In Mark 16:15, Jesus' last words were "Go into all the world and proclaim the good news to the whole creation." In Luke 24:47, 49, Jesus' last words were "repentance and forgiveness of sins is to be proclaimed in his name to all the nations... stay here... until you have been clothed with power from on high."

We have been given the power of the Holy Spirit to transform the world for Jesus. We have the same power the early church had. But here is the key: We must do something with this power! When Jesus said, "Go and make disciples..." he was giving the Great Commission. It was not the great reflection. It was not the great suggestion or the great option. It was the Great Commission. It is a mandate from Jesus

Christ. Jesus made no distinction between his followers and his witnesses. Discipleship and evangelism cannot be separated. A faith worth having is a faith worth sharing.

This is the rub of the faith, isn't it? It is easy to come to worship and Bible study. It is even easy to serve the church in some way. But sharing our faith? That is another matter. Many want to leave that job to someone else.

A while back my wife and I were having dinner with some friends at a new restaurant. The food and service were fantastic, but there were not many people at the restaurant. A friend of mine spoke up and said, "We have to tell more people about this place. It is great and nobody is here. It would be a shame if they went out of business."

I am a preacher and I am always thinking. How quick we are to share something good. We will tell everyone about a good restaurant or a good book. When we see a good movie we will tell the whole world to go see it. When we find a good deal somewhere we will sky write it. Yet when it comes to sharing the greatest news in the universe, mum is the word for many Christians.

I love the story found in the first chapter of Acts. Jesus is ascending into heaven and Jesus' followers are looking up in awe. As Jesus is ascending he is telling his followers to "go and be witnesses..." And his followers just keep looking up. When Jesus disappears, two men appear and basically say, "Stop looking up into heaven. Did you hear what Jesus said? Go and be witnesses!"

I know many Christians who are looking up instead of looking out. Jesus is telling us today, "Stop looking up; look out! I'm out there, waiting on you to help me change people with my love. Be my witnesses. Stop looking up! Look out! I am out here in the world with those who are suffering and I need for you to be my hands and feet! Will you help me?"

Perhaps you are thinking, "Yeah, but sharing faith is so personal." You bet it is. The consequences of sin are personal.

Living with no hope is personal. Living life with no meaning or purpose is personal. It is a personal tragedy. We have been given the power to transform people with God's love. We have the source of hope and strength. Will we share it? If we had the cure to cancer we would tell everyone. We have the cure for a meaningless life and spiritual death. What's keeping us from sharing it?

I know that the word "witness" conjures up many negative images. I know that many people have given the word "witness" a bad name. We think of people passing out tracts, holding up signs, grabbing people by the lapels, and screaming about Jesus with judgment in their eyes. Quite often those who loudly profess to follow Christ don't behave like Christ.

Shane Claiborne, a wonderful new Christian writer and thinker, talks about walking into downtown Philadelphia with some friends and watching the magicians, performers, and artists perform on the streets. They came across this preacher who was standing on a box screaming into a microphone. Beside him was a coffin with a fake dead body inside. He talked about how everyone was going to die and go to hell if they didn't know Jesus. All Shane could think about doing was jumping on a box beside him and yelling at the top of his lungs, "God is not a monster!"

We are fond of quoting John 3:16, "For God so loved the world..." But the Bible also says in John 3:17 that God did not send Jesus to condemn the world but to save it! It is high time Christians start believing it and, more importantly, living like it!

The more I read the Bible and the teachings of Jesus the more I see Claiborne's assertion: "Christianity spreads not through coercion or force, but through fascination." People are fascinated by the love of Jesus. When we are reflecting that love, people want to know about it. First Peter 3:15-16 says it well: "Always be ready to make your defense to anyone who demands from you an accounting for the hope that is in you; yet do it with gentleness and reverence." It is so simple. When we are filled with the hope and love of Christ, people will want to know about it. We live in a world filled with people who have no hope and so when others see our hope, they are drawn to us. When we are living out the love of Christ, we will not need to seek out people and tell them about Jesus. They will seek us out!

A few years ago something fascinating happened at a high school in Unionville, Tennessee. Three nominees for homecoming king decided that if one of them was awarded the crown they would give it to a junior named Scotty Maloney, who has Williams syndrome, a neurological disorder that affects learning and speech. When Jesse Cooper's name was called as the winner at a ceremony, the principal announced what the nominees decided to do. "I've been blessed with so many things," Cooper told ABC News' Nashville affiliate WKRN-TV. "I just wanted Scotty to experience something great in his high school days." "When they called Scotty's name, his eyes got really big and I don't know that he registered exactly what was happening. He knew something was," Maloney's teacher Liz Hestle Gassaway told ABCNews.com. "It was very, very emotional." The crowd erupted with cheers and Maloney got a long-standing ovation, WKRN reported, as he was awarded his "king" medal. Everyone loves Maloney at that school. He wears that medal wherever he goes.

That's the kingdom folks. That fascinating love made headline news! When we embody the love of Jesus it will get people's attention. When every Christian embodies the fascinating love of Christ, the world will want to know about it and they will want it too!

If you are looking for more motivation read the last chapter of John. In that final chapter we read that Jesus was eating breakfast with Peter and Jesus asked him, "Peter, do you love me?" Peter, somewhat surprised by the question, replied, "Of course, I love you, Lord." Jesus said, "Then feed my sheep." Jesus asked Peter this question a second and a third time and after Peter affirmed his love, Jesus' response was always the same, "Feed my sheep." If we love Jesus, then we will feed his sheep. Do you love Jesus? For goodness sake, don't keep it to yourself. Share that love. The world needs it desperately. Can I get a witness? Amen.

Epiphany 3
Ordinary Time 3
Mark 1:14-20

Now after John was arrested, Jesus came to Galilee, proclaiming the good news of God, and saying, "The time is fulfilled, and the kingdom of God has come near; repent, and believe in the good news." As Jesus passed along the Sea of Galilee, he saw Simon and his brother Andrew casting a net into the sea — for they were fishermen. And Jesus said to them, "Follow me and I will make you fish for people." And immediately they left their nets and followed him. As he went a little farther, he saw James son of Zebedee and his brother John, who were in their boat mending the nets. Immediately he called them; and they left their father Zebedee in the boat with the hired men, and followed him.

The Great Omission

As Christians, we only have three things that are required of us: love God, love our neighbor as ourselves, and make disciples. To make disciples means to be witnesses of Christ in order to bring others into a relationship with Christ. When Jesus called Simon and Andrew to follow him he was very clear, "Follow me and I will make you fish for people" (Mark 1:17). The call to make disciples was clear from the start of Jesus' earthly ministry through the very end. In fact, at the end of Matthew before Jesus ascends to the Father, Jesus' last words to his followers were no, "Go and find a comfortable church and have covered dish dinners." His last words were not, "Go and sing the songs you like in worship." He didn't say, "Be good little boys and girls. Stay out of trouble." He didn't say, "Keep in touch through prayer as often as you can" or "Don't skip church too often." He does not say, "Try to do some good every once in a while." No. What does he say? "Go and make disciples!"

This is called the Great Commission, not suggestion, but commission! The church is the only institution in the world that exists for those outside of it. Unfortunately, many churches don't even see it as a suggestion. Instead, it has become the Great Omission. Many churches have lost sight of the mission to make disciples. This is one of the reasons why the mainline church is struggling. The mainline church is not replenishing itself with a new generation of disciples. We are not reaching the younger generation. Fewer and fewer churches are bringing even one new person to Christ in one year.

What has happened? Why can't today's church be like the early church? The answer comes through something that A.W. Tozer said long ago: "If the Holy Spirit was withdrawn from the church today, 95% of what we do would go on and no one would know the difference."

Is the Holy Spirit the driving force of the church today? If we are to reclaim the fire of the Spirit the early church had, we must get back to fundamentals — what we believe and what we practice. We must be willing to open ourselves to the movement of the Holy Spirit. That's what the early followers of Christ did. They were not sophisticated people. They hadn't been to seminary. They hadn't read books on church growth and marketing. They simply made themselves available to the Holy Spirit. Look what happened: "Each one heard them speaking in his own language" (Acts 2:6 NIV).

This was not the gift of tongues, or the gift of *glossolalia*. What's happening here is not speaking in unknown tongues. That is another theological issue. What's happening here is that a bunch of people from all over the place, all speaking different languages, all coming from different cultures, heard the gospel in their own language. The good news of the saving love of Jesus Christ was communicated to them! It was clear! The followers of Christ were not multilingual! The Holy Spirit did it through them because they were simply willing to be used! The Holy Spirit broke through communication barriers and the gospel translated.

Isn't it interesting that here in our post-modern world with all of our miraculous communication technology we still have communication problems? Isn't it interesting that in spite of our advances in Bible translations and production of gimmicks that people are still turned off by religion and the church? It seems we are good at information but not communication.

Will Willimon once wrote, "To many outside the church, the church is like a football huddle. You know that something important is being said there, but you can't understand a word of it, and all you can see is their rear ends." How is it that the early church was able to communicate so clearly and we have so much trouble? The answer is revealed through a humorous but painfully true cartoon in the *Leadership Journal*. The church secretary is holding the phone, hollering to the pastor in the adjoining room. She says, "A man from *Ripley's Believe It or Not* wants a picture of someone on fire for the Lord. Do we have one?"

Where is our love for God and our passion and love for people? This is what translates! When you forgive while everyone else wants revenge, that translates. When you are loving while everyone else is hateful, that translates. When you don't give up on people when everyone else wants to, that translates.

There is a great debate in the church on how to be relevant in this post-modern world. Because the mainline church is struggling to grow we are falling all over ourselves trying to reach the next generation. I went to a meeting about this very thing. We talked about gimmicks, models, and strategies. There is a place for all that but sometimes I wonder with Howard Olds whether we are trying so hard to be "with it" that we just "don't get it." We need to be in touch with the world, not in sync with the world.

The church ought to be a little weird. We ought to be a little off-kilter. If people come because the values of the world have diminished them and they are looking for something different, why would they be attracted to us if we are like the world? So if we are a little odd or a little weird, that's good. It is as if we are saying, "What you are looking for you will not find in the world!" People respond to real people who have a real love and passion for God. The gospel does not have to be dressed up, dolled up, or given a makeover. The gospel does just fine by itself.

The early church knew this. The power of the early church was rooted in prayer and discernment from the Holy Spirit. When we follow suit and truly seek the Spirit we will start addressing the real spiritual needs of people and when we do that, people will start listening to the church.

I like the story Wayne Cordeiro tells about a bakery located in a city where he used to live. It was in a bad part of town. The bakery was small, rundown, and nondescript. Yet at 5 a.m. every morning the aroma of delicious bread emanated from that bakery. People would line up around the block to get their hands on that bread. That is a parable for us as the church. It is not about appearances or gimmicks; it is simply about offering the bread of life. People are so hungry spiritually that all we have to do is offer the bread of life with passion and authenticity and they will come from all over to taste it. Does the sweet smell of Christ emanate from your life? Are you sharing your witness? Are you letting your light shine?

The unavoidable truth is that as Christians we are called to bear witness to the hope that is within us — to tell people about Jesus — to make disciples. This may scare some of you to death. But take heart. By the grace of God, you are able to preach. You don't do it on your own power. This is why Jesus said, "I am with you always, to the end of the age" (Matthew 28:20). Jesus is always with us, helping us and empowering us to share the good news. I know he is. As a pastor, I have heard many great sermons from ordinary people. The church is filled with wonderful preachers.

I remember hearing a minister talk about a parishioner who worked with a young man still living at home. The young man was rather quiet and this parishioner did not know him that well. One day he found the young man crying in the restroom. He asked if he could help. The young man confided in him. He said that his girlfriend was pregnant and he had just revealed this to his parents the night before. They screamed at him and said that he had embarrassed them. They said he had shamed the family and told him that he should never set foot in their house again.

What did this parishioner do? He reached out, put his arm around him and said, "I am sorry that happened to you. I am sure this is difficult for your parents, and I am certain this is difficult for you. But I am a Christian, and I believe that God loves you, and his love will help you through the most difficult situations."

How was he able to say something like that? Jesus said, "Go and make disciples and remember I am with you always."

Will Willimon had a parishioner who was very close to someone who was terribly depressed. She could understand the reasons for her depression. She had just lost her job, her mother had just died, and a long-term relationship she had been in had recently ended. However, she felt that her friend's depression had reached a dangerous level. She suggested to her friend that it might be a good idea to see a counselor. Then, in the middle of sharing coffee, she felt led to say to her friend: "I guess we have never talked about something like religion or spirituality, but I want you to know that I believe that Jesus Christ is more than an idea. He is a presence. He loves you very much and because he has helped me through so many crises in my own life, I believe he can help you through this crisis. Would you like to pray together?" So they prayed. After the prayer, her friend said that the prayer helped.

How was she able to be so bold with her friend? Jesus said, "Go and make disciples and I will be with you always."

One time I preached at a youth camp. The chapel service went really late. I didn't get up to preach until about 11 p.m. It didn't help that I had the flu. But it was the last service of the week and I had to finish. I don't know what I said. I was so sick. I was just trying to get through it. I thought it was the worst sermon I ever delivered.

After the service a teenage girl approached me. She looked very angry. She said, "I have to find out if something is true." I replied, "What's that?" She said, "You mentioned tonight that God loves me. Do you believe that? I don't believe anyone has ever loved me. My dad left me and my mother abused me, and I moved from one institution to another. I've been sexually abused, neglected, and you are telling me that God loves me?"

I looked into her eyes and said, "That's right. I know this for certain. God loves you. You want to know how I know? God got up on a cross and said, 'This is how much I love you.'" She paused for a moment and tears began rolling down her cheeks. Then she said, "Well, if God loves me, then nothing else matters. If God loves me, that's all that matters."

Deep down you know there are people all around you who need the love, forgiveness, grace, power, strength, and comfort of God in Jesus Christ. Give one good reason why you wouldn't want to share it. Amen.

Epiphany 4
Ordinary Time 4
Mark 1:21-28

They went to Capernaum; and when the sabbath came, he entered the synagogue and taught. They were astounded at his teaching, for he taught them as one having authority, and not as the scribes. Just then there was in their synagogue a man with an unclean spirit, and he cried out, "What have you to do with us, Jesus of Nazareth? Have you come to destroy us? I know who you are, the Holy One of God." But Jesus rebuked him, saying, "Be silent, and come out of him!" And the unclean spirit, convulsing him and crying with a loud voice, came out of him. They were all amazed, and they kept on asking one another, "What is this? A new teaching — with authority! He commands even the unclean spirits, and they obey him." At once his fame began to spread throughout the surrounding region of Galilee.

Defeating Discouragement

Yard sales are interesting to me. I don't frequent them very often, but I am always fascinated by the fact that "one person's trash is another person's treasure." Someone can't wait to get rid of old tapes and records — doesn't want them cluttering up the house anymore. Along comes a complete stranger and he just can't believe anyone would want to sell them. He buys them for a steal and drives home with a big smile thinking he just committed robbery. He brings the records home, clutters up his own house with them, and he's as happy as can be. Human beings can be strange sometimes.

Satan once had a yard sale. He thought he'd get rid of some of his old tools that were cluttering up his house. There was gossip, slander, adultery, lying, greed, power-hunger, and lust laid out on the tables. Interested buyers were perusing the tables looking for a good buy.

One customer, however, strolled way back in the garage and found on a shelf a very shiny tool. It looked well cared for. He brought it out to Satan and asked if it was for sale. "Oh, no!" Satan answered. "That's my tool. Without it I couldn't wreck the world! It's my secret weapon!" "But what is it?" the customer inquired. "It's the tool of discouragement," the devil said.

Nothing takes the life right out of you more than discouragement. A discouraged spirit is a powerless spirit. It is an awful feeling — it feels like the wind has been knocked out of your soul.

I'm sure that is how the man possessed by an evil spirit felt when he met Jesus. He was so discouraged that he was too blind to see that Jesus wanted to heal him of his demons. The gospel of Mark states that Jesus told the man to be quiet and then ordered the evil spirit to come out of him. If we could just quiet the demons within us that bring discouragement that easily. Sometimes it is hard to do.

She lost her job at the agency three years ago. This tough economy has made it difficult for her to find a job. She has managed to make ends meet waiting tables. She often cries herself to sleep at night thinking that three years ago she had a corner office. Now, she has a sore back from cleaning tables. She doesn't know how much longer she can do it. There is discouragement.

They were happily married for twenty years, or so he thought. He came home one day and she was gone. There was a note on the kitchen table that read, "I don't want to be married to you anymore." It took his breath away. He can't wrap his mind around it. He hasn't slept in weeks. There is discouragement.

She loved where she used to live. She had lots of friends and a great school. But Daddy needed to find work elsewhere. So they moved far away. Different school. Different neighborhood. Different culture. They make fun of her accent at school. She can't find anyone to sit with at lunch, so she eats her lunch alone on a hard bench outside. She hides her tears as people walk by. There is discouragement.

Discouragement is an awful thing. Life pulls the rug right from under you, and you have nothing to hold onto. Your confidence is shattered. A sense of well-being is a distant memory. Your motivation has evaporated. Have you ever felt that way? If you have, do you remember how you got over it?

Some people never do get over it. A traumatizing event occurs, discouragement sets in, and they are never the same.

Every day is a battle with discouragement. They just can't seem to get over what happened to them. In every circumstance, they are a victim. In every relationship, they are a victim. In every conflict, they are a victim. Do you know anybody like that? Discouragement is a strong force.

We've all been discouraged. We know how debilitating it can be. I've always wondered why some people seem to bounce back from it while others wallow in it forever. I know people who have gone through unspeakable things throughout their lives and they just keep on going and never miss a beat. I know others who experience one set back in life and they live in the pit the rest of their lives.

I have always been curious as to what makes that difference. That wouldn't be a bad research project — why some people get over discouragement and disappointment and others don't. What's the difference? Genetics? Upbringing? Mental attitude? Religion? A change in lifestyle?

Maybe that's it — a change. When you're discouraged nothing seems better than change, any change, anywhere other than where you are and what you are feeling. I know a lot of people who think change is the answer. If you have a bad experience at work, quit and go look for another one. If you are disappointed in your spouse, call the divorce attorney. Are you disappointed in your friends? Cuss them out and go find new ones. Are you discouraged by the way you look? Get plastic surgery.

I heard about a middle-aged woman who had a heart attack and was taken to the hospital. While on the operating table she had a near-death experience. During that experience she saw God and asked if this was it. God said, "No, you have another thirty years to live."

Upon her recovery she decided to just stay in the hospital and have a face lift, liposuction, Botox, tummy tuck, the works. She even had someone come in and change her hair color. She never liked the way she looked, so she figured since she had another thirty years she might as well make the most of it.

She walked out of the hospital after the last operation and was killed by an ambulance speeding by. She arrived in front of God and complained, "I thought you said I had another thirty years." God replied, "I didn't recognize you."

Maybe making a drastic change isn't always the answer to discouragement! You know, sometimes making a lot of changes can be a form of running away. But we can't run away from our feelings or from who we are. Running away never solves anything.

The Bible has a lot of wisdom. It probably would not be a bad idea to consult the Bible on an issue like discouragement. And you know who I think would be a good person to ask about how to get over discouragement? Isaiah. Isaiah was very wise. Isaiah knew about discouragement. The prophet wept over the suffering of Israel. Isaiah saw the coming of the Babylonian army and watched as they destroyed Jerusalem. The prophet, along with the rest of God's people, was held captive and he watched as his nation was ruined. His heart sank as he watched God's people become discouraged and bitter. He was called to encourage the people of God.

Yeah, I think Isaiah would be a good person to seek advice from about discouragement. I believe the wisdom he gave to the beat-up nation of Israel is good enough for us today:

> Have you not known? Have you not heard? The Lord is the everlasting God, the Creator of the ends of the earth. He does not faint or grow weary; his understanding is unsearchable. He gives power to the faint, and strengthens the powerless. Even youths will faint and be weary, and the young will fall exhausted; but those who wait for the Lord shall renew their strength, they shall mount up with wings like eagles, they shall run and not be weary, they shall walk and not faint.
> (Isaiah 40:28-31)

That sounds more like it, doesn't it? That's what we need — to run and not be weary, to walk and not faint — to soar like an eagle. Have you ever seen an eagle fly? It is one of the most beautiful sights in the entire world! The eagle spreads its wings, exerting very little effort, allowing the wind to carry it along as it climbs higher in the sky. Wouldn't it be great to live life that way? I know many people who would love to live life that way. I know people in the pit who would love to soar like an eagle. Are you one of them?

I'm glad Isaiah mentions walking and not fainting. So much of life is about walking, going one step at time. Someone once said that "the problem with life is that it is so daily." It is true, day after day, one little thing after another, life is so daily. Yet Isaiah says we can have sustaining strength that empowers us day after day.

That's sounds wonderful, doesn't it? I want to have that kind of energy and strength in life! So, how do we get it? Isaiah tells us exactly how to get this kind of power for living. It is right there in the text. The key is right under our nose. I'm going to tell you what it is, and it can change your life.

Before we can truly hear and apply the key to power for living, we have to embrace an eternal truth that people trip over all the time. It is our unwillingness to accept this truth that causes so much of our suffering and our inability to get over discouragement. Ready? Here it is: Anyone who seeks to live by their own power will eventually break down. Isaiah put it this way, "Even youths will faint and be weary and the young will fall exhausted." Count on it. No matter how young you are, how self-sufficient you may be, or how independent you may feel, if you try to live your life on your own power, you will break down. You will fail. You will give out. You will be discouraged over and over again.

This is a truth so many of us resist. We don't want to be told that we can't stand on our own two feet. We don't want to be told that we can't handle life on our own. We don't want to be told that we are vulnerable.

A few years ago pop singer Madonna did the half-time show at the Super Bowl. It was quite a spectacle. *Vogue* magazine gave the show rave reviews. You know why they thought the show was so good? Because, for a moment, they felt that Madonna looked like she was in her twenties again. Our culture does not like to hear that "youth will faint and be weary and the young will fall exhausted," but it is true as the day is long.

It is only when we stop resisting this truth that we open ourselves to the power over discouragement. What is that power? It is the power of God! If there is one thing this passage teaches us, it is that God has power and God gives power. Isaiah tells us that God gives power not to those who think they are strong, not to those who pull themselves up by their own boot straps, not to those who think they can handle life on their own, not to those who are proud of their fragile self-sufficiency. Isaiah says God gives power to the weak, the vulnerable, the open, the powerless, the willing, those who are yielding to him.

If you are discouraged today, the worst thing you can do is to try to overcome by sheer will power. The best thing you can do is what Isaiah directs us to do: "Wait for the Lord." Now, this is not a passive, lazy waiting. This is a hopeful waiting, a purposeful waiting. It is a waiting that knows in God's good time God will provide God's good answer. This is a waiting that holds on for God's response. Some call it faith.

Unfortunately, faith is misunderstood. So many people see faith as simply a means to end — faith is crossing our fingers to God and hoping hard enough that things turn out the way we want. And when they do, well, we had faith. That's not faith. Someone once said that "faith is not the means by which we achieve victory; faith is the victory itself." Victory is achieved when we trust God's timing and wait hopefully for him. Victory over discouragement is achieved when we stop rushing ahead of God, quiet our hearts before him, and wait for his strength.

Some of you may be thinking, "Okay, I've got my Bible open on my lap and I'm saying, I am waiting on you, God. Is that it? Is that all I have to do?" Well, it is not a bad start, but there is a little more to it than that. The key that unlocks God's soaring power in your life is found in one little word in verse 31 — "renewed." In Hebrew the word literally means "exchange" — to exchange one thing for another — to hand God one thing and receive something else from him — to let go of one thing and gain something new. According to Isaiah, God's strength comes only when this exchange is made. We have to give something up. We have to make room for God's strength.

Now, what in the world do you think we would have to give up in order to gain God's strength? Can't we just get God's strength? Would you believe there are obstacles in our lives that hinder our ability to receive God's strength? Would you believe there are things that clutter up our souls so much that there is no room for God's strength? For some it is pride. For others it is control. Still, for some, it is a sinful habit which diminishes them but they can't seem to let it go.

A few years ago my friend and his family were on vacation in Sweden. One day they went to a children's zoo. They had a great time, but while my friend was in the zoo he witnessed something very strange. He watched as little kids with pacifiers in their mouths dropped their pacifiers into this big pit. One by one they would come and drop their binkies, and then they would start crying and reach back for them. My friend was more than curious, so he walked up to the pit and saw hundreds of pacifiers on the ground. He was baffled, so he asked an attendant who spoke English what was happening. The attendant told him it was "pacifier heaven." The attendant went on to tell him that within that particular town in Sweden there is a long-standing tradition that when kids are at an age when they need to give up their pacifiers, the family takes them to "pacifier heaven," and they give them up.

It is time to give up the pacifier of control. It is time to stop trying to live life on our own power. It is time to stop pushing our agenda over God's agenda. You want to soar like an eagle? Give up your control for God's control.

Give up the pacifier — exchange your weakness for God's strength. Amen.

Epiphany 5
Ordinary Time 5
Mark 1:29-39

As soon as they left the synagogue, they entered the house of Simon and Andrew, with James and John. Now Simon's mother-in-law was in bed with a fever, and they told him about her at once. He came and took her by the hand and lifted her up. Then the fever left her, and she began to serve them. That evening, at sundown, they brought to him all who were sick or possessed with demons. And the whole city was gathered around the door. And he cured many who were sick with various diseases, and cast out many demons; and he would not permit the demons to speak, because they knew him. In the morning, while it was still very dark, he got up and went out to a deserted place, and there he prayed. And Simon and his companions hunted for him. When they found him, they said to him, "Everyone is searching for you." He answered, "Let us go on to the neighboring towns, so that I may proclaim the message there also; for that is what I came out to do." And he went throughout Galilee, proclaiming the message in their synagogues and casting out demons.

Does Prayer Make
Any Difference?

I want to address a subject that many of us struggle with — prayer. Deep inside many of us want to know if prayer makes a difference. And if it does make a difference, what difference does it make? Does prayer really work? If it does work, how does it work?

Those of us who are Christians know that prayer is something we ought to do. If we need something — if we are confused about something — if we need guidance or direction — we have been taught to pray about it. In fact, most of us have heard well-meaning friends ask us, "Have you prayed about it?"

You know that prayer is important but maybe you struggle with prayer because you never seem to get the results you are looking for. You know you need to take time to talk with God but it just doesn't seem to get you anywhere. You know you need to pray but you just don't seem to get an answer. Maybe this frustrates you because you hear people talk about the power of prayer like God is eating cornflakes with them at the breakfast table every morning and when you pray it feels like you are ringing the door bell to an empty house.

Maybe you are someone who has a heavy burden or a serious issue in your life and you have prayed repeatedly about it and you wonder if all your prayers are falling on deaf ears. Maybe you have prayed for a troubled child, a sick relative, a job, a better marriage, or some other serious issue and you don't seem to be getting the answer you need. You wonder,

"Is God listening?" Maybe you feel you are not doing it right and you think if you buy the latest book on prayer or attend a conference you can find the right prayer technique that will "open sesame"!

Perhaps you find the act of praying difficult because you get easily distracted and bored. "Okay God, here I am, I have this need and…. Is God really listening or am I just talking to myself? … I do need to get to the grocery store… There is that email I need to return…. Well, I can always pray later. After all, this is God. He knows me. He knows my thoughts before I think them. Why do I have to pray when he knows what I am going to say? I can be doing something more productive with my time…" Can you relate?

Some of you may be skeptical about prayer. Maybe you think it is just wishful thinking or whistling in the dark. You think the whole idea of the Creator of the world listening to one prayer among billions is ridiculous. "Really? God has to listen to so many prayers! How does that work?"

Does prayer make any difference or are we just wasting our breath? Does prayer matter or are there better things we can do with our time? So much of our frustration with prayer has to do with a lack of understanding of what prayer is. Is it religious magic? Is it giving a cosmic Santa Claus a list? Is it putting our order into the universe? Is it crossing our fingers Christian style? What is prayer really? Until we understand what prayer is we will never understand the huge difference it can make in our lives.

I want to help you understand what prayer is and how to do it. Prayer is the single most important act for anyone who seeks to follow God. We can't know the will of God for our lives unless we pray. We can't be strong in the face of temptation unless we pray. We can't be the people God wants us to be unless we pray. We can't be healthy spiritually unless we pray. We can't make lasting changes in our lives unless we pray. We can't get faith right until we get prayer right.

Jesus knew this. Jesus understood the importance of prayer and the difference it makes. Jesus prayed all the time. In the first chapter of the gospel of Mark we find that Jesus woke up exhausted from all the healings he did the day before. We are told that he sneaked away to a quiet place and prayed. He had a demanding job and needed to pray as often as he could (Mark 1:35). In fact, in the gospel of Luke we find fifteen different references to Jesus praying! At every turn in his life and ministry Jesus was praying. He prayed as he began his ministry. He prayed to renew himself. He prayed before he chose his disciples. He prayed as he evaluated his ministry. He prayed as he served and healed people. He prayed as he faced his crucifixion. He prayed on the cross. He prayed after he was resurrected. Jesus was always praying. It wasn't an option for Jesus. He knew that in order for him to accomplish what God wanted him to do, he needed to pray. If Jesus thought it was that important to pray, don't you think we should be praying?

In Luke 11 we notice the disciples picked up on Jesus' habit of praying. They saw him praying all the time and thought that they could learn something from it. So one time when Jesus was praying in a certain place, the disciples approached him and asked, "Jesus, that prayer thing you are always doing? Can you teach us to do it too?" Jesus agreed and began to teach them. First he gave them a powerful prayer to learn — the Lord's Prayer. After that, he taught them about the importance of prayer. Please understand — this teaching was not from a prayer guru who had written a best-selling book. This was a lesson on prayer from Jesus himself.

Then Jesus told his disciples a parable about the importance of persistence in prayer (Luke 11:5-8). Jesus underscored that the key to effective prayer is to pray persistently and habitually. Are we surprised? If I go to the gym once a month, do you think it will do me any good? If I follow my diet once a week, do you think it will do me any good?

Prayer works the same way. For prayer to make a difference it must become a habit.

Many of us forget this simple truth. We pray for something once and we are disappointed when nothing changes. Perhaps we think, "Doesn't God hear me the first time?" Yes, God hears us the first time, but prayer is deeper than that.

Next Jesus basically tells them that God always answers our prayers (Luke 11:9-11). Whenever we ask, God will answer. Whenever we search, we will find. Whenever we knock, God will open the door. Jesus says this is true for everyone. Everyone who seeks God persistently in prayer will receive an answer. This is a spiritual law. God answers prayer. The power of God through prayer is available to everyone.

Notice what Jesus did not say in this text. Jesus did not say everyone who asks receives the answer they want, finds what they are looking for, or has the door they want open opened. God always answers us, but we may not always like the answer or expect the answer we get. What we want from God and what we receive from God are two different things. God loves us too much to always give us what we want because sometimes what we want is not good for us or what is best for us, but God will always answer us.

Jesus clearly states that there is something we can always count on to receive from God when we pray. Jesus says that whenever we seek God in prayer, God will always give to us the Holy Spirit (Luke 11:11-13). What is the purpose of the Holy Spirit? To love us, mold us, shape us, guide us, empower us, and direct us. This means that prayer is not putting our order in to God. It is not rubbing a magic lamp or giving a Santa Claus in the sky our list. Prayer is not getting our phrasing right so we can unlock the God machine. Prayer is the one essential practice that brings us closer to God and allows us to be formed by his love. Prayer is not "getting" from God; prayer is *intimacy* with God. Prayer is developing a relationship with God. That's why it must be a habit.

Prayer is not meant to persuade God; it is meant to change us. Prayer does not give us what we want from God; prayer helps us want what we need from God. What we need is to get our hearts right. What we need is to get our souls right. What we need is to get our relationships right and this can only happen through a relationship with God in prayer.

The truth is that most of the time we don't want a relationship; we want a road map. We pray, "Okay God, I don't need much of your time. You don't need to get too involved. Just give me some direction here. What should I do?" God replies, "Just hang out with me for a while. Let's spend some time together. I want to show you some things." We persist, "Lord, really. I don't need that much of you. Just give me a yes or no." God replies, "Just abide in me and my love from day to day and you will find what you are looking for."

God still wants us to bring him our needs, our desires, and our questions and doubts. God loves us and wants us to give him all that we are but the answer to our questions, needs, and desires comes as we develop an intimate relationship with God through prayer. When we develop intimacy with God through prayer, we find that abiding in his love and being the people he wants us to be is where true life is found. The more we experience true life the more we want to please God. And the more we want to please God the easier it is for us to change. And the easier it is for us to change the quicker we are to pray, "Lord, I want to fit into your plans."

Do you want God to move like a tidal wave in your life? Do you want prayer to make a huge impact in your life? Be prepared to pray, "Lord, whatever you want, that's what I want too!" When you are ready to surrender like that in prayer, life gets exciting and becomes more interesting than you would ever imagine. You see, we must move from

"Lord, this is how I want things to work in my life" to "Lord, I want what you want for my life."

If you desire intimacy with God through prayer today, I have a simple suggestion for you. If you do what I am about to suggest you will experience the difference that prayer can make in your life. For the next seven days start your day with prayer. It doesn't have to be a long time, just five to ten minutes. You can stay in your bed, sit in a chair, or do it at the breakfast table. Get a devotional or turn to your favorite passage of scripture. Read the devotional or scripture passage. When you find that you are quiet on the inside, pray, "Lord, I want to get to know you better. I want to know your love. I want a relationship with you." Then share with God what is on your mind and heart. Don't hold back. Just share it. He is listening and wants to hear from you. Be sure to include not only your own needs but the needs of others. Before you end your prayer time, pray, "Lord, I want to please you. I want to do your will. Whatever it is you want, that's what I want too. I want to fit into your plans. Show me the way."

Jesus knew the power of submitting to God's will. Perhaps Jesus' most important prayer was the one he prayed in the Garden of Gethsemane. His capture and crucifixion were close at hand. He was emotionally and spiritually exhausted. He was tempted not to go through with God's plan. He pleaded with God to let the "cup" pass from him. It was at that moment when he said the prayer that changed everything — "Lord, not my will but yours be done." This was not Jesus' first prayer to God. He had been praying his whole life and ministry. He had developed such love and trust for God that when it came to the moment of truth, he was prepared to surrender to God's will. As a result, the world was changed. It is my assertion that what enabled Jesus to do what God had sent him to do for the world was his consistent prayer life throughout his ministry.

Just imagine how close you could feel to God if you prayed more. Imagine what God could show you if you prayed more. Just imagine what God could do through you if you prayed more. Imagine the strength and wisdom you could have if you prayed more. Imagine the opportunities from God that would open for you if you prayed more. Imagine the person you could become if you prayed more. Imagine the relationships that could be healed if you prayed more.

Imagine the impact your church would have if everyone in your congregation developed the habit of prayer. Imagine the lives you could touch for Christ if you prayed more often. Imagine. Amen.

Epiphany 6
Ordinary Time 6
Mark 1:40-45

A leper came to him begging him, and kneeling he said to him, "If you choose, you can make me clean." Moved with pity, Jesus stretched out his hand and touched him, and said to him, "I do choose. Be made clean!" Immediately the leprosy left him, and he was made clean. After sternly warning him he sent him away at once, saying to him, "See that you say nothing to anyone; but go, show yourself to the priest, and offer for your cleansing what Moses commanded, as a testimony to them." But he went out and began to proclaim it freely, and to spread the word, so that Jesus could no longer go into a town openly, but stayed out in the country; and people came to him from every quarter.

Unstoppable Love

If I could only preach one sermon, my point would be Jesus loves us more than we could ever imagine and wants to bring healing and wholeness to our lives. I have been preaching the gospel for over twenty years. During that time I have learned one indisputable fact: Only the love of Christ can satisfy and sustain us.

Jesus Christ is in love with the world and desires more than anything else for us to receive his forgiveness, grace, power, and love so that we can live an abundant life.

To drive this point home, I want to take a closer look at a moving passage in the first chapter of the gospel of Mark when Jesus healed a leper. There are a few critical ideas in this passage that all of us need to remember about Jesus and his love.

A leper approached Jesus and said, "If you choose, you can make me clean" (v. 40). Jesus said, "I do choose" (v. 41). Other translations have Jesus saying, "I am willing" (v. 41 NIV). Jesus is willing and able to bring his love into our lives. His love can transform, guide, and comfort us. All we have to do is receive it. Jesus' love is available.

The fact that Jesus' love is available may seem obvious. However, it has been my experience that many people see the love of Jesus as something beyond their reach, reserved for holy people or something they have to earn. You hear it in the language of people: "Lightning would strike if I went to church." Unfortunately, some Christians have not helped to discourage this attitude. They look like they were baptized in lemon juice and have nothing but judgment for the world.

I remember playing golf with a friend who said to me, "Say a good word for me to God. Life has been tough lately." I replied, "Hey, why don't you talk to him yourself? He loves you and wants what is best for you. The question is will you let him love you?" He was silent the rest of the round. You could tell it never occurred to him that God was ready to listen to him and help him.

You see, it is not a question of whether or not Jesus is willing to love us; the question is will we allow his love and presence to be the dominant force in our lives? Jesus' love is the only real love that is truly available and reliable for any of us but it takes some folks a long time to learn it.

Ask the world, "Will you love me?" The world will reply, "Sure, as long as you are successful and don't disappoint us." Ask your workplace, "Will you love me?" Your workplace will reply, "Sure, as long as you show up on time and improve the bottom line." Ask the economy, "Will you love me?" The economy will reply, "Sure, as long as you have a job and can pay your bills." Ask the culture, "Will you love me?" The culture will reply, "Sure, as long as you stay young and do everything you can to impress others."

It is amazing to me how many folks will continue to look for love in all the wrong places. As a minister I have a front row seat to people's lives and I have never seen a job, a toy, a house, or a romance bring the kind of joy, healing, and power that comes through a relationship with Jesus Christ. I have never had anyone come back to me and say, "I tried a relationship with Jesus and it just does not do it for me." But I have had people say, "Jesus has changed my life. I wouldn't be the same without his love."

Jesus' love is available! The leper knew this. There was something about Jesus that told him Jesus was the only one who could make him whole again. Leprosy was an awful disease. It caused the skin to develop terribly painful repulsive sores. Back in Jesus' day if you had leprosy and were near others who didn't have the disease, you were obligated to shout "Unclean! Unclean!" A rabbi especially was not to go near lepers because he was required to obey certain Jewish laws regarding cleanliness. So it took great courage for this leper to even approach Jesus. He did so because he knew that Jesus could give him the healing love he so desperately needed.

Maybe you feel like that leper. You feel left out, picked on, and pushed aside. You feel ugly. You are desperate for a healing love that will show you your worth and make you whole. The good news is Jesus is walking by. He is right there beside you. You don't have to beg like the leper. All you have to do is say, "Lord, I need your love and grace. Come and make me clean and put a new spirit within me." If that is your desire, Jesus will be overjoyed, and he will shower you with his mercy and grace.

Our text in Mark says that when Jesus was moved with compassion he reached out and touched the leper. He touched him. Back then they didn't know much about leprosy. The Jews thought if someone got leprosy it was because of some grievous sin. Lepers were unclean and if you touched a leper you also became unclean.

Yet Jesus reached out and touched the man. He didn't heal him and then touch him. Jesus touched him and his touch healed him. It was Jesus' personal touch that healed him.

With maybe two or three exceptions, Jesus always healed with a personal touch. This is critical for us to remember. Jesus' love is available and it is personal. This means Jesus loves the world in general but he also loves the world in particular. Jesus loves each one of us personally and desires to touch us and communicate with us personally. We serve a personal God. God takes things personally! The gospel of John says, "And the Word became flesh and lived among us" (John 1:14).

I recall having a conversation with someone who had just received Christ as Lord and Savior and joined the church. She said, "Before I never really understood it. But now I get it. He loves me personally. Jesus wants a relationship with me."

Our relationship with Christ is personal. Everyone's relationship with Jesus is different. Because Jesus' love is personal, he is going to connect with us and we are going to connect with him in different ways. He knows us better than we know ourselves. What is good for one person is not good for another. Our relationship with Jesus is custom made.

Someone once said that the two most important days of your life are the day you were born and the day you discover why you were born. A relationship with Jesus brings those two pivotal days of your life into focus. Jesus empowers us to live our lives with purpose and meaning.

Jesus' personal touch should remind all of us who are in ministry that our ministry should also be personal. If I was to teach a class in seminary for pastors, it would be about how to build relationships. We are called to relate to people personally because that is what Jesus did. Committees and structures have their place but if we ever lose the personal touch of compassion that Jesus embodied, the church will cease to make an impact on this world.

I have found Facebook and Twitter to be great ways to connect with people. I think Jesus would have used Facebook. However, social media will never replace personal touch and connection. In fact, I remember getting a message on Facebook that read, "Can't wait to see you in person!" Enough said.

My advice is that from time to time we need to take our eyes off of a screen and look into the eyes of the people we love and offer the personal touch like Jesus. Jesus is our best model. He never stopped reaching out to others in love. He still does today.

In the story of Jesus healing a leper there are two ways we see that Jesus' love is unstoppable. The first is through the man's response to Jesus' healing. I think it was the human side of Jesus that thought this man could keep his healing quiet. Remember, Jesus was human and divine. In Mark Jesus is understood in light of the cross. Jesus wanted to be sure people understood him not just by his healings but by his ultimate act of love on the cross.

But who was Jesus kidding? This man had been healed by Jesus' love! This was like telling a sewing circle not to share gossip. There was no stopping the news of Jesus' love and power! The healed man told everyone and everyone flocked to Jesus. That is a great picture. The best advertising is word of mouth, and the best evangelism is word of mouth — telling others what Jesus' love has done for us.

When the love of Jesus gets hold of us, there is no stopping it. We want to tell others and show others what his love has done for us. I can preach about sharing our faith, but the better part of me knows that when Jesus gets hold of people I will not have to tell them to share it. It will be unstoppable.

The other way we see that Jesus' love is unstoppable is through his audacious act of crossing the cultural taboo of leprosy. Lepers were unclean, condemned to live away from the community. They were even separated from their own families. They couldn't worship with their faith community. They were completely ostracized. Yet Jesus disregarded the taboo and loved this leper. Jesus was always disregarding cultural boundaries and rules, especially when it came to relating to people. He reached out to hated tax collectors, oppressed women, and unclean lepers. He healed on the sabbath and didn't care which laws he broke. For Jesus, love is the highest law. Jesus' love is unstoppable and limitless. It knows no bounds. Nothing can stop the love of God!

Our culture has its own version of lepers today. We often set up boundaries and taboos against those we misunderstand, fear, or hate. Some of us think that Jesus' love stops short of them but we are wrong.

A colleague of mine loves to tell the story about a woman who was active in his church who had a husband who was an atheist. He would come to worship with her occasionally to support her but he thought faith in God was just a fairy tale. Not long after she became active in the church, her husband was stricken with cancer. She loved him and cared for him as he became weaker and closer to death's door.

Before he died he received Christ as his Lord and Savior. When he was asked what convinced him to believe in Jesus, his answer was quite surprising. It was not because of a thoughtful sermon he heard or because of an astute theological argument. He said he became a Christian because of the way his wife loved him and cared for him during his battle with cancer. He commented that he always heard about the love of Jesus and thought it was a nice idea. But when he experienced the loving way his wife held him and comforted him even though he didn't believe, he knew in his heart Jesus' love was real.

Jesus' love is available, personal, and unstoppable. It knows no bounds. It crosses cultural taboos, touches the untouchable, and makes believers out of atheists. Amen.

Epiphany 7
Ordinary Time 7
Mark 2:1-12

When he returned to Capernaum after some days, it was reported that he was at home. So many gathered around that there was no longer room for them, not even in front of the door; and he was speaking the word to them. Then some people came, bringing to him a paralyzed man, carried by four of them. And when they could not bring him to Jesus because of the crowd, they removed the roof above him; and after having dug through it, they let down the mat on which the paralytic lay. When Jesus saw their faith, he said to the paralytic, "Son, your sins are forgiven." Now some of the scribes were sitting there, questioning in their hearts, "Why does this fellow speak in this way? It is blasphemy! Who can forgive sins but God alone?" At once Jesus perceived in his spirit that they were discussing these questions among themselves; and he said to them, "Why do you raise such questions in your hearts? Which is easier, to say to the paralytic, 'Your sins are forgiven,' or to say, 'Stand up and take your mat and walk'? But so that you may know that the Son of Man has authority on earth to forgive sins" — he said to the paralytic — "I say to you, stand up, take your mat and go to your home." And he stood up, and immediately took the mat and went out before all of them; so that they were all amazed and glorified God, saying, "We have never seen anything like this!"

Prayer Changes Things

Dr. Arthur Caliandro, long-time pastor of Marble Collegiate Church, had a therapist on his church staff. One day they were having a conversation about prayer. The therapist told him that prayer was the most therapeutic behavior for a human being. Caliandro was not surprised but he was excited because an expert in human behavior was telling him what he knew all along — prayer is powerful!

Do you desire power for living? Try prayer power! In Acts we read that in God "we live and move and have our being." You see, we as human beings are not electrically powered, computer powered, hydraulically powered, or mechanically powered. We are God-powered! In Genesis it tells us that when God created us, he breathed his life-breath into us. Therefore, we must go to God as often as we can to receive the breath of life.

Jesus knew the power of prayer. The gospels demonstrate that prayer was the power source for Jesus' ministry. Luke 5:16 (NIV) states that Jesus "would withdraw to deserted places and pray." The Greek word "withdraw" means "he continually withdrew." In other words, withdrawing to pray was his habit. Indeed, it was. In the gospel of Luke we find fifteen different references to Jesus praying. We find that Jesus prayed at every turn in his life. He prayed as he began his ministry. He prayed before choosing his disciples. He prayed as he served others. He prayed as he faced temptation and difficulty. He prayed at his death. He prayed after his resurrection. This begs the question: If Jesus, our Lord and Savior, believed prayer was this important for his own ministry, then shouldn't it be just as important to us?

There is power in prayer. I remember the pew pencils in my church growing up. They had three simple words on them: "Prayer Changes Things." Prayer does change things. When did we ever lose sight of that? Some of us don't give prayer the time we give our cup of coffee in the morning. Make no mistake. Prayer changes things.

I recall being called to the hospital when I served a church in another city. A good friend of mine by the name of Howard was very ill. He had a blockage in his intestines and had developed a bad infection. It did not look good. I arrived at his room and we visited for a little while. He was very weak. I then asked if I could pray for him. He agreed. I put my hand on his shoulder and I remember a conflict going on between my head and my heart. In my head I remembered all my seminary training that taught me not to raise hopes in my prayers for those who are sick. I was taught to put caveats in my prayers. Well, my heart wanted to do something different. My heart wanted to ask God to heal Howard. My heart won the battle. I prayed boldly, "Lord, heal Howard of this affliction."

A week or so later guess who walked into my office? Howard! He sat down and began to cry. He said, "I have been healed and I believe your prayer healed me. I don't know if you felt it, but when you prayed for me I felt a warm wave come through your arm and hand and into my body. This was when my healing started."

I don't claim to be a faith healer but I do claim this: There is power in prayer! Howard's experience taught me this again. This experience also taught me that we need to take a second look at how we pray. Many of our prayers are simply anemic. We put caveats in them like, "Maybe Lord, if it be your will, then…." Too often our prayers sound like we are trying to give God an out or preventing God from being embarrassed. God does not need for us to give him an out or protect him from embarrassment.

C.S. Lewis said, "When we get to heaven we will find that many of God's 'no's' were really God's 'yes's'." In hindsight, we have all experienced the relief that comes when God does not answer our prayers in the way we want but God never told us to quit praying! I've come to the place in my life where when I want something from God, I boldly ask God for it. Now, if God does not want me to have it, then God won't give it to me. I won't be upset. God knows what is best but I still pray boldly. God likes bold prayers. The Bible is filled with bold prayers.

I get weary of wimpy prayers. The book of James says that we "have not because we ask not." Psalm 37:4 says, "Take delight in the Lord, and he will give you the desires of your heart." Jesus tells us in John that if we "abide in him" he will give to us what we ask. We read these passages and believe them, but then we just pray for our hangnail or the callus on our foot. We need to come to the place where we trust God to answer our prayers. We need to pray big, bold, Bible-filled prayers and understand there is risk in prayer. I believe we will be judged by the size of our prayers. We serve a prayer-answering God.

Recently, the Roman Catholic church approved a new iPhone "App" (application) for confessions. You can just type in your confessions on your phone and be absolved. How convenient. You know what I thought when I heard about this? Big deal! I have had an "app" like this long be-fore there were cell phones. All of us have this "app" and it costs us nothing. We don't need a cell phone or computer to use it. All we have to do is get on our knees. This "app" is prayer! The Bible tells us that if we confess our sins to God in prayer, God will forgive us.

We don't need an iPhone app to learn how to pray. We don't need a book to tell us how to pray. We don't need to go to a seminar, retreat, or conference to learn how to pray. We don't have to go to seminary to learn how to pray. All we need to do is pray! God is delighted whenever and however we seek him. The best way to learn how to pray is to pray. The Spirit will help us find our way.

If you need a tangible method to prayer then try what I like to call the TALK method. TALK to God. The first T is for thanksgiving. Begin your prayer time with *thanksgiving* to God. Share with God for what you are thankful. This begins your prayer time with a spirit of praise and joy for all that God has done and draws you closer to God. The A stands for *ask*. Ask God for what you need and want. Be bold and specific. Don't worry. If God does not want you to have something, he will not give it to you. But ask for it. If it is in God's will, he will provide what is needed for you to have it. Remember in your asking to not only pray for what you need but for the needs of others. We have a God who answers all of our prayers. The L stands for *listen*. After you have made requests to God, then spend time just listening to God. This takes practice but once you get the hang of it, it becomes the most powerful part of prayer. Finally, the K stands for *keep a journal*. Keep a prayer journal and write down what you are learning in your prayer time. Also, keep scripture passages in your journal to refer to during your prayer time.

We need to remember that the same God who created the universe is waiting to hear from us. The same God who parted the Red Sea is waiting to hear from us. The same God who enabled David to defeat Goliath is waiting to hear from us. The same God who raised Jesus from the dead is waiting to hear from us. The Bible tells us that faithful praying can move mountains!

You want to know how to get your prayers answered? We find the key in Mark 11:24 when Jesus says, "So I tell you, whatever you ask for in prayer, believe that you have received it, and it will be yours." There are three things in this text that we must do to get our prayers answered. First, we need to be specific. Jesus says, "Whatever you ask for...." Prayers need to have a target. If you need something, ask God for it. Don't feel selfish or ashamed. Think of it this way — oftentimes we don't discover what we really want until we begin to pray for what we want. God will work things out for us. If God does not want us to have what we are asking for then God will not give it to us. God will give us something better.

Second, pray with passion. Jesus says, "Believe you have received it...." Wimpy prayers don't move mountains. Remember when Jesus healed the daughter of the Syrophoenician woman. Jesus said to her, "Never in all of Israel have I seen faith like yours."

Third, pray with faith. Did you notice the verb endings in this verse? They are in the past tense. They have already happened. So often God is ready to give us something and God is just waiting for us to get ready for it and ask for it. As the old saying goes, "When the student is ready, the teacher will appear."

One of the greatest examples of the power of faith is seen in the second chapter of Mark when four men never gave up on bringing their paralyzed friend to Jesus. They carried their friend on a mat to a home where Jesus was teaching. The crowd surrounding Jesus was so large they could not even get in the front door. But they did not give up. They had faith that they could get to Jesus and he could heal their friend. They climbed up on the roof of the house and dug a hole through it and lowered their friend down to Jesus. Jesus was so impressed with their faith that he forgave the paralytic's sins on the spot and told him to get up and walk. He got up and walked right out of the house! Praying with faith is powerful. Don't ever give up on your prayers.

There is one more thing we must do if we want God to answer our prayers. It is in Mark 11:25, "Whenever you stand praying, forgive, if you have anything against any-one...." The biggest block to answered prayer is a resentful heart. If you are choosing not to forgive someone, remember you are poisoning your soul and preventing God to move in your life and answer your prayers. If you are having trouble forgiving someone, then try praying for them every day. It is difficult to stay angry at someone you are praying for every day. Soon your attitude toward the person will change and the big mountain of resentment in your heart will dissolve. There is power in prayer!

Back in the mid 1800s there lived a man by the name of Alfred Nobel. He invented a revolutionary new chemical. It was an explosive that could be kept safe until it was time to ignite it. Nobel was a Christian and understood some biblical Greek. He decided to name his new chemical *dunamis* or dynamite. His vision came from Mark 11:23 where Jesus tells us that faithful praying can move mountains. This is exactly what dynamite originally did. It removed mountains so highways could be built! Nobel became very wealthy, as you might imagine. He set up a foundation. Perhaps you have heard of it — The Nobel Prize.

We have our own spiritual dynamite. It is called prayer and it can move mountains. There is power in prayer. It is the power source. Use it. If you hold on to God through prayer you will find that prayer does indeed change things.

You want more proof? Here is a portion of an email I received from a young lady who learned the power of prayer:

My name is Tamara. I'm 32 years old and I used to work at Channel 10 in St. Petersburg as the news producer of the 6 p.m. show. I now live in Atlanta and work for CNN.

I have never considered myself very spiritual/religious even though I've always believed in God. But two years ago, give or take a few months... I found your church as I was heading to the beach one afternoon. From the very first time I attended I not

156

only left inspired and uplifted from your words, but I remembered what it was like to truly feel God in my life again. I hadn't felt that in years.

In June of 2012 I was diagnosed with Acute Myeloid Leukemia. I am doing great and will beat this! My older sister was a perfect donor match and in seven days I find out if I'm in remission, which right now is looking pretty darn good! I have a lot to be thankful for and God has truly blessed me. He never gave up on me!

After being diagnosed... for a while I couldn't pray. I didn't know what to say. I was angry, confused, and I didn't understand. I was a healthy, happy 32-year-old, my career was finally where I wanted it to be... how could this happen?

I don't remember a lot about being in the hospital during my treatment.... I think I've tried to block out the long days... but I do remember watching one of your sermons one day or night while I was in there and I can honestly say that it brought me back to God. I guess I could say... it brought my faith back into my heart. I can't even tell you what the sermon was about, I can only tell you that you touched me once again... inspired me and uplifted me in a very dark place. After that I started to pray again and haven't stopped since.

I've kept in touch with Tamara since I received that email and she is now cancer free. She is happy, healthy, and prays every day. She says the source of her strength in good times and in bad is the time she spends with God in prayer. Prayer changes things. What are you waiting for? Start praying! Amen.

Epiphany 8
Ordinary Time 8
Mark 2:13-22

Jesus went out again beside the sea; the whole crowd gathered around him, and he taught them. As he was walking along, he saw Levi son of Alphaeus sitting at the tax booth, and he said to him, "Follow me." And he got up and followed him. And as he sat at dinner in Levi's house, many tax collectors and sinners were also sitting with Jesus and his disciples — for there were many who followed him. When the scribes of the Pharisees saw that he was eating with sinners and tax collectors, they said to his disciples, "Why does he eat with tax collectors and sinners?" When Jesus heard this, he said to them, "Those who are well have no need of a physician, but those who are sick; I have come to call not the righteous but sinners." Now John's disciples and the Pharisees were fasting; and people came and said to him, "Why do John's disciples and the disciples of the Pharisees fast, but your disciples do not fast?" Jesus said to them, "The wedding guests cannot fast while the bridegroom is with them, can they? As long as they have the bridegroom with them, they cannot fast. The days will come when the bridegroom is taken away from them, and then they will fast on that day. No one sews a piece of unshrunk cloth on an old cloak; otherwise, the patch pulls away from it, the new from the old, and a worse tear is made. And no one puts new wine into old wineskins; otherwise, the wine will burst the skins, and the wine is lost, and so are the skins; but one puts new wine into fresh wineskins."

Learn to Play Again

A group of theologians and scholars once cornered C.S. Lewis and asked him, "What is the most important theological discovery you have ever made?" Lewis smiled and responded, "I exist to enjoy God's enjoyment of me." Did you know that? God enjoys you! God wants you to enjoy him, to enjoy life, to enjoy the world he has created, and to enjoy the people he has put in your life. Scripture backs up God's call to enjoy life in 1 Timothy 6:17 (NIV):

> Command those who are rich in this present world not to be arrogant nor to put their hope in wealth, which is so uncertain, but to put their hope in God, who richly provides us with everything for our enjoyment.

A long, long time ago a group of people in the church got together and thought it was important to make a list of the most important beliefs of Christianity. They called it "catechism." They soon discovered that the list was too long and difficult to memorize, so they came up with a "short catechism." This was to be a summary of the key beliefs of our faith. Do you want to know how this shorter catechism begins? "What is the chief end of humankind? To glorify God and enjoy him forever!"

I come across so many people who won't allow God into their lives because they think God is going to make them give up fun. Many misguided Christians have perpetuated this nonsense. They give off the impression that to become a Christian means the party is over — that being spiritual means being miserable. Nothing could be further from the truth. In fact, to become a Christian means the party is just beginning. When you have the joy of Christ in your heart you can't help but smile and have a good time. My number one rule for the staff of my church is to have fun. Ministry is supposed to be fun. I have the most fun job in the world! I get to tell people how much God loves them and that God's love can help them live better lives. How much fun is that?

God created us to play and to enjoy the life he created! I would go so far as to say that God requires us to have fun. The Bible tells us so. In the tenth chapter of Mark we read that Jesus was teaching and a bunch of playful kids ran toward him. The sour disciples were appalled. You can imagine their reaction, "Children ought to be seen and not heard. Where are their parents? Can't they see these kids are interrupting Jesus? Get these kids out of here!" The Bible says that Jesus became very angry at the disciples. He felt the kids were treated unfairly. He said, "What are you doing? Let the children come to me. Don't get in their way. In fact, unless you can receive the kingdom like these kids, you will never be able to enter it."

What did Jesus mean by this bold statement? Children are receptive, dependant, and trusting. They bring nothing but themselves and their joy. Jesus says that unless we are able to receive God and his kingdom like children, we will never understand life and God.

G.K. Chesterton was a profound Christian writer who inspired C.S. Lewis. He wrote something that I have never been able to forget. He wrote that "God is the last child left in the universe." He said the rest of us have just lost our joy. I believe Chesterton was on to something. When we read Genesis we see that joy radiated through God as he created the universe. When God created you and me there was great joy in his heart. For example, do you think when God thought about creating a daisy, he just said, "Um, daisies be"? I don't think so!

Tony Campolo talks about the time when his grandson was just a little boy and would play on Campolo's knee. He would bounce him up and down, lift him up into the air, and bring him down to the ground. Campolo said that every time he would do this his grandson would say, "Do it again, Pop! Do it again!" And Campolo would do it again. Of course, his grandson would say to him once more, "Do it again, Pop! Do it again!" Campolo says that when God created that first daisy something childlike inside the heart of God said, "Do it again! Do it again!" And after the fourth and fifth daisy God said to himself, "Do it again! Do it again!" And after the fifty billionth, trillionth daisy God was jumping up and down, clapping his hands saying, "Do it again! Do it again!" We have a God of joy, fun, and play!

But something happened to our world. We lost our joy. We lost our sense of fun and laughter. Sin and cynicism crept in and caused us to lose our ability to play. God wanted us to get our joy back, so he decided to come to us in Jesus Christ. One of the things God said to us in Jesus was, "I came that they may have life, and have it abundantly" (John 10:10).

In Jesus God was showing us his joyful personality so that we would get our joy back. At first, the world really did not know how to respond to this. We see an example of this in Mark 2 and Luke 7 when Jesus spoke to the Pharisees, the supposed experts of the Jewish Law. They thought they knew everything there was to know about God. Jesus came along and said, "You just don't get it. I come eating, drinking, and having a good time and you accuse me of being a glutton, drunkard, and a friend to sinners and tax collectors." Someone once said that basically Jesus was accused of being a party animal! They thought Jesus was playing too hard. They thought they knew everything about God. They thought God was not into fun, games, and play, but they were wrong. They just could not see that Jesus was trying to get us to enjoy life again.

Do you know what Jesus' first miracle was in John? It occurred in a small town called Cana at a wedding party. A wedding party back then could go on for an entire week! Jesus was invited to this party. One of the first scenes of Jesus in John is not him preaching a sermon or holding a sick person's hand; it is Jesus at a party! After a few days they ran out of wine. What do you think Jesus did? Help clean up and say goodnight? No! He told some folks to fill several large jars with water and he performed his first miracle by turning all that water into wine. So Jesus' first miracle in John was not healing the sick, feeding the hungry, walking on water, or raising the dead. His first miracle was making gallons of wine so a party could continue!

You can read the story of Jesus turning the water into wine over and over again. You can read every biblical commentary on the planet. You can ask biblical scholars and theologians to explain the story with some profound theological point, but you will never find what you are looking for because the great truth of that story is this: Sometimes Jesus enjoyed having fun! Jesus was showing us how to get our joy back and for our joy to be full.

I think of it this way. When I was a little boy and would get grumpy and grouchy, my dad had a clever way of changing my mood. He would not lecture me. He wouldn't tell me that I should be grateful for what I had and not complain. He would get on the floor with me and find a place just above my belly button and blow air bubbles on my tummy. He would do it until I smiled and gave into laughter. Quite simply, this is what God did for us in Jesus. God got down on our level and embraced us so that we might get joy back in our lives.

You have homework to do. Go out and let yourself be loved. Go hack at a golf ball. Take dance lessons and learn how to dance. Turn on your favorite song and sing like no one is listening. Go watch your favorite comedy and laugh your way to joy!

Norman Cousins was a great doctor who found that there was healing power in laughter. In fact, laughter saved his life. He was at death's door and decided to find a bunch of episodes of *Candid Camera*. He watched them over and over again and laughed his way back to health!

I came across a wonderful quote from an 85-year-old woman from the hill country of Kentucky:

> If I had to live my life over again, I would dare to make more mistakes next time. I would relax. I would be sillier. I would take fewer things seriously... I would eat more ice cream and less beans. I would have more actual troubles but fewer imaginary ones... if I had to do it over again, I'd travel lighter.

What would you say if you had to finish this sentence: "If I had to live my life over, I would..."? Don't wait to experience God's joy in your life. Do it now! Learn to play again. Every moment is a gift. This is why we call it "the present."

Enjoy God's enjoyment of you. Enjoy your life, have fun and play. When you do, you will be very close to the kingdom of God. Amen.

Epiphany 9
Ordinary Time 9
Mark 2:23—3:6

One sabbath he was going through the grainfields; and as they made their way his disciples began to pluck heads of grain. The Pharisees said to him, "Look, why are they doing what is not lawful on the sabbath?" And he said to them, "Have you never read what David did when he and his companions were hungry and in need of food? He entered the house of God, when Abiathar was high priest, and ate the bread of the Presence, which it is not lawful for any but the priests to eat, and he gave some to his companions." Then he said to them, "The sabbath was made for humankind, and not humankind for the sabbath; so the Son of Man is lord even of the sabbath."

Again he entered the synagogue, and a man was there who had a withered hand. They watched him to see whether he would cure him on the sabbath, so that they might accuse him. And he said to the man who had the withered hand, "Come forward." Then he said to them, "Is it lawful to do good or to do harm on the sabbath, to save life or to kill?" But they were silent. He looked around at them with anger; he was grieved at their hardness of heart and said to the man, "Stretch out your hand." He stretched it out, and his hand was restored. The Pharisees went out and immediately conspired with the Herodians against him, how to destroy him.

True North

Sha Jahan was the emperor of India during the 1600s. When he lost his wife he was devastated. In fact, his grief was so great that he decided to build a grand temple that would serve as her tomb. Her coffin was placed in the center of a large piece of land and a big temple was built around it. The emperor was determined to build a magnificent resting place for his wife.

However, as the weeks turned into months the emperor's grief was overshadowed by his passion for the project. He was obsessed with the construction. One day, while walking from one side of the construction site to the other, he tripped over a wooden box. In frustration he ordered that the box be thrown out. What he did not realize was that he had ordered the disposal of his wife's coffin. The person the temple was supposed to honor was forgotten, but it was built anyway.

This story haunts me. Could someone build an elaborate tribute and forget the hero? Yes, it can happen. The scary thing is that it can happen to our faith. It is possible to practice faith and forget who we put our faith in. It is possible to sing the hymns and forget the one we are singing to. It is possible to say a prayer and forget who we are praying to.

It's possible to get lost in the midst of our faith. In fact, it has been my experience that sometimes those who seem to have the strongest faith are the most lost. Sometimes in our ambition to follow God we forget who God is, what God wants us to do, and why he wants us to do it. We stumble. We make mistakes. Our relationships get tangled up. We find ourselves in a mess wondering how we got so lost. We went to worship. We read the Bible. We prayed. We thought we were doing the right thing. We followed the rules. Where did it all go wrong? How did it get so confusing? How did we stray so far from the path?

Maybe you made a decision thinking it was the right thing to do and it has just made things worse. Maybe you said something you thought needed to be said and it blew up in your face. Maybe you have done something you thought would please God and now you know in your heart you should have handled things differently. You have hurt yourself and others.

Living out our faith in this messy world can be difficult. It is easy to lose our way. This is why from time to time we need to find "true north" for our faith (actually I mean "magnetic north" but true north sounds better!). A compass always points to magnetic north to help us travel in the right direction. The good news is Jesus gave us "true north" in his teachings. When we are lost and confused all we have to do is remember Jesus' most important lesson and we can get on the right path again.

We get lost when we forget this lesson from Jesus. We can study the Bible and still get lost. We can go to worship every week and still get lost. We can follow the rules and behave and still get lost. We can look religious, keep our noses clean, and follow all ten of the commandments and still miss who God is and what his desire is for us.

In the second chapter of the gospel of Mark we see an example of how the most religious people can be the most lost. The Pharisees were chastising Jesus' disciples for plucking the heads of grain to eat on the sabbath. According to their strict interpretation of the law, the Pharisees considered this work and no one was allowed to work on the sabbath. Jesus told them to get some perspective. He mentioned a time when David broke ceremonial law to feed hungry people. He told the Pharisees, "The sabbath was made for humankind, and not humankind for the sabbath" (Mark 2:27).

We can get spiritually lost like the Pharisees if we don't remember Jesus' most important lesson. If you will take this lesson to heart it will never fail to guide you. If you will remember this lesson you can always find your way back home. If you will internalize this lesson from Jesus, your faith will always find the path that God desires. Take this compass to work where things get difficult and confusing and you will find clarity. Take this compass when you are out with friends and family and see the difference it makes in your relationships. Keep this compass with you when you are with your spouse and experience the happiness of your marriage increase. Keep this compass with you at all times and watch your life take on new meaning and significance.

So let's find "true north" for our faith. Let's find our internal compass from God. We find it in chapter 22 of the gospel of Matthew. Jesus had just finished debating the Sadducees, the wealthy Jewish aristocrats. They tried to stump Jesus with theological questions but Jesus' answers rendered them speechless.

It was now the Pharisees' turn to test Jesus. As we saw earlier in Mark, the Pharisees were experts in the Jewish Law. They knew the law backward and forward. They classified over 600 laws and often listed them in order of importance. They loved to debate which laws were the most important. One Pharisee said sarcastically, "Well if this Jesus of Nazareth is so smart surely he can tell us which law is the most important of all." He was trying to test Jesus:

> When the Pharisees heard that he had silenced the Sadducees, they gathered together, and one of them, a lawyer, asked him a question to test him. "Teacher, which commandment in the law is the greatest?"
> (Matthew 22:34-36)

Now, count on a lawyer to stir the pot and cause trouble! You can hear the sarcasm, "Teacher, which commandment is the greatest?" He thought, "I got him. No matter what he says he's going to be trapped. He can't get this right! If he says one rule is more important, people are going to get mad that he is disregarding all the other laws."

The Pharisee was a lot like people today who see religion as a set of rules and laws and God as the punisher of those who break the rules. I know many folks who grew up thinking that religion was about following the rules and staying out of trouble. "Don't do this and don't do that!" Maybe you sat in church terrified. Maybe you went to private religious school and have bad memories of teachers punishing you for being bad. Maybe you still find it hard to shake those memories and those ideas about religion. Perhaps you have family and friends who haven't darkened the door of a church in years because of such memories.

Ironically, Jesus was the greatest rule breaker in history! That's what got him killed! You don't get flogged and crucified for following the rules. For example, Jesus broke another rule when he responded to the Pharisee's question. The response Jesus gave astounded the Pharisees:

> Jesus said to him, " 'You shall love the Lord your God with all your heart, and with all your soul, and with all your mind.' This is the greatest and first commandment. And a second is like it: 'You shall love your neighbor as yourself.' On these two commandments hang all the law and the prophets."
> (Matthew 22:37-40)

Jesus' answer was revolutionary. He quoted from Deuteronomy 6:5 and Leviticus 19:18. He said if someone follows these two commands he or she will keep the essence of the law. Jesus was saying, "You want the CliffsNotes™ version of the law? You want me to sum it up for you? You don't have to memorize all these little rules and laws and worry yourself sick. All you have to do is two things and you have it. Here it is: Love God with all your being and love other people like you would love yourself. You do that you have the law down."

You can see the Pharisees' jaws drop. They had dedicated their lives to poring over 613 laws. They interpreted them and debated them. Along comes this carpenter from Nazareth and he wraps them all up in one sentence!

The Pharisees were so preoccupied with the details of the law that they failed to see the heart of the law. Jesus was a master at bringing out the heart of the matter. His answer shows us that the purpose of the law is to bring us closer to God and our neighbor. If we love God and our neighbor we are fulfilling what God desires. That's it! That was the heart to all of it.

One time the Pharisees chastised Jesus and his disciples for breaking a dietary law. Jesus told them to get some perspective. He said it is not what you eat that makes you unclean; it is what comes out of your mouth that makes you unclean. In other words, it is what is in your heart that matters.

The Pharisees had lost their way. They had good intentions. They wanted to follow the law but in their desire to do so they missed that the point of all those laws was to love God and one another. They missed the forest for the trees. In trying to fulfill the law they were disregarding their love for God and others. Sound familiar?

So many Christians get lost putting rules, doctrine, theology, and judgments over loving God and neighbor. They start off with good intentions. They take a stand and express their position. But often over time their position, theology, and ideas become more important than their relationship with God and others. It can happen to all of us. What troubles me about the Christian church today is how often we put interpretations of our faith over the heart of our faith. Theology and interpretation are important but they never supersede the greatest commandment.

I knew a guy when I was in college who would debate anybody on theology and the Bible. He would take on anyone who disagreed with him. One day we were sitting at a table in a courtyard and he was debating with this guy. They had a class together and were always disagreeing with each other. He said something to my friend that got him really angry. My friend went off on him, "The Bible says... The Bible says..." He was almost screaming. When he was done pontificating, his classmate looked at my friend and asked, "Why do you hate me so much?" My friend stuttered, "I, I, I don't hate you... I just disagree with you." His classmate replied, "I've never been able to tell the difference." Then he walked off. I have never forgotten the lesson I learned that day.

Jesus said that people will know we are his followers not by our hatred, not by our judgments, not by our theology, not by our pride, not by our interpretation of scripture, but by our love for one another. In glory, God is not going to say, "Well done child, you were correct in the way you interpreted the book of Revelation... Well done child, you were part of a denomination that was my favorite... Well done child, your theology was perfect." No, God is going to say, "Well done child, you loved me with all of your heart and you loved my children."

Love is the highest law! Can you imagine how much energy the church would save and could use for better purposes by embracing Jesus' call to release judgment and love the world? Imagine all the energy that is wasted when Christians have crusades against something. Imagine saving that energy and using it for ministries and causes that infuse the world with the love of Jesus!

If the church spent as much energy taking care of the poor as we do on justifying prejudice, the world would be a different place. If the church spent as much time loving the least, last, and lost as we do on crusades against something, the world would be a different place. If the church spent as much time bringing healing and compassion to those who are suffering as we do on debating the interpretation of scripture, the world would be a different place. If Christians spent as much time loving God as we do condemning those who sin differently than we do, the world would be a better place.

Jesus' true north (the greatest commandment) does not contain the words "don't" or "should not" anywhere. Following God is not about not doing this or not doing that; it is about *doing all we can* to love God and others. Those who follow Christ are not worried about what they should not do; they are focused on what they *can do* for God and what God can do through them. Christ's followers should not be known by what they don't do but by what they do! Christ's followers should not only be known by what they are against but by what they are for!

How do we use this compass in our daily lives? How do we find true north as we go to work and school, deal with deadlines, kids, bills, in-laws, and annoying neighbors? Well, it is pretty simple. Before you speak at a pivotal moment — before you make a decision — before you choose a path — before you respond in the heat of the moment — before you make a business transaction ask yourself, *"Will this honor God? What is the loving thing to do?"* Ninety-nine percent of the time you will be confident about your decisions and actions if you ask these two questions. And that one percent? Well, if you happen to face that one percent call a pastor or counselor and ask them to help you.

One of the things I do is ask myself these questions before I begin my day. During my quiet time with God in the morning I ask myself, "How will I honor God today? How will my words and actions be a reflection of love to those around me?" Those questions have gotten me out of more trouble than you can imagine!

But the days I am rushed and I skip that quiet time, I don't ask myself those questions and my day is off-balance. I don't have the clarity I need. It is not as if God is not with me; it is that my heart has not been prepared for the day. And when our hearts are not prepared every day to honor God and love others, then our days can become a trip without a compass.

Think of professional athletes. Have you ever gone to a major league baseball game and arrived before the game started? What did you see? You saw the players on the field contorting themselves in all kinds of positions. You saw them sprinting all over the field. What were they doing? They were stretching and warming up. A professional athlete would never start playing a game without first warming up.

Spending time with God is our time to stretch our souls and warm up our hearts before God. It prepares us for our day. Christ's followers should never begin a day without first warming up before God. This is how our souls become sensitized to God's guidance each day.

Imagine how different your days would be if you were guided by the greatest commandment. Imagine the change in your attitude when you truly love God with all your being each day — when your heart feels God's love, when your soul is guided by God's love, and when your mind thinks and meditates on God's love. Imagine the healing that would come to your relationships when you choose to do the most loving thing to others. Imagine the joy, meaning, and significance that will come into your life when you live on God's wavelength.

Will this honor God? What is the loving thing to do? Those two questions will change your life. Amen.

Transfiguration of Our Lord
Mark 9:2-9

Six days later, Jesus took with him Peter and James and John, and led them up a high mountain apart, by themselves. And he was transfigured before them, and his clothes became dazzling white, such as no one on earth could bleach them. And there appeared to them Elijah with Moses, who were talking with Jesus. Then Peter said to Jesus, "Rabbi, it is good for us to be here; let us make three dwellings, one for you, one for Moses, and one for Elijah." He did not know what to say, for they were terrified. Then a cloud overshadowed them, and from the cloud there came a voice, "This is my Son, the Beloved; listen to him!" Suddenly when they looked around, they saw no one with them any more, but only Jesus. As they were coming down the mountain, he ordered them to tell no one about what they had seen, until after the Son of Man had risen from the dead.

The Cost of Discipleship

I get a kick out of bumper stickers. Whenever I see an interesting one I always take a glance at the person who is driving the car. I want to get a glimpse of the person who would drive around with a crazy bumper sticker. I'm sure I am not the only one who has ever done that!

Here are a few bumper stickers that I have seen or heard about over the years that always make me laugh:
• What If The Hokey Pokey Is What It's All About?
• Driver Carries No Cash — He's Married!
• I'm Retired — Go Around Me!
• Normal People Scare Me!
• Save Our Planet — It's The Only One With Chocolate!
• I Get Along With God Just Fine; It's His Fan Clubs I Can't Stand!
• Do You Follow Jesus This Close? (for the English teachers, it should read "closely")

That last one is a good one. It's funny but like all good humor there is an element of truth to it. From time to time we need to examine how closely we are following Jesus. We talk a big game about Jesus. We ask, "What would Jesus do?" We want to be like Christ. We claim to be followers of Christ but how closely are we following him and what does it mean to follow him?

Mark's account of the Transfiguration is a good example of how misguided we can sometimes be about following Jesus. Jesus took Peter, James, and John up a mountain for a spiritual retreat. Jesus started to glow and Elijah and Moses appeared to them. Peter thought it would be a good idea for all of them to stay up on that mountain and he even offered to help build a house for all of them. It's kind of funny when you think about it. Peter must have thought it was cool to be up there with Jesus, Moses, and Elijah. Why not stay there forever and not deal with the realities of life? What Peter did not realize was that the special moment on that mountain was not about escaping the world on a retreat; it was about God confirming once again that Jesus was his Son and he would die and then rise from the dead. As they followed Jesus back down that mountain he tried to tell them, but they still did not understand. They did not understand that they were following a man who would die and then live again and if they were serious about following him, they would have to die too.

Following Jesus is the greatest thing in the world but it is also the hardest thing in the world to do. Following Jesus is more than showing up to worship one hour a week. Following Jesus is more than throwing money in the plate every once in a while. Following Jesus is more than reading the Bible occasionally. Following Jesus is more than letting someone in front of you in traffic. Most people don't realize that when Christ calls people he calls them to come and die. What many don't understand is that to experience the abundant life in Christ, we have to take up a cross and die.

Jesus was clear about this from the very beginning. Huge crowds followed Jesus wherever he went. There was this certain energy about him. More than likely, he had charisma. He had a way with words. He performed miracles. He challenged people in authority. He loved everyone, especially the left out, thrown out, and the down and out. Who wouldn't love a guy like that?

One day Jesus looked over a huge crowd that was following him and he wondered if they really knew what it meant to follow him. Then with no regard for what is taught in a

Dale Carnegie course on "How to Win Friends and Influence People," Jesus spoke some of the hardest words we find anywhere in the gospels. He said, "Do you really want to follow me? Consider what it is going to cost you. You must give up everything that is dearest to you, take up a cross, and follow me. Unless you do that, you cannot be my disciples."

That is not what the crowd wanted to hear. They thought this magnetic man was on his way to his own empire. They hoped that if they followed him they would share in his power and glory. What they did not realize was that when Jesus said these words he was on his way to Jerusalem — to the cross, and to follow him meant you were also willing to take up a cross. The Bible does not mention it one way or the other but I imagine that after Jesus spoke these words most people in the crowd fell back from Jesus, disappointed and dejected.

I suspect that most of us are like that crowd. Most often we follow Jesus from a distance. We seek Jesus for the perks and benefits. We want to be on the hopeful side of things. We want to have good morals and values. We want to have someone we can pray to when we need help or need a miracle. We want our eternal salvation to be secure. To be sure, there is nothing wrong with any of these things, but we are not always prepared to follow Jesus closely because we know it will cost us.

The truth is that important, sacred, and virtuous things in life have a cost. The glowing bride and excited groom stand before me at the altar. The bride is thinking, "Oh, this is the man of my dreams. He is going to bring me flowers every day. He is going to know what I am thinking and know exactly what to say. He is going to hang on my every word and always be patient with me. He will always just want to cuddle. He is going to rub my feet whenever I ask and surprise me with breakfast in bed." The groom is thinking, "Oh, this is the woman of my dreams. She is always going to look this young and beautiful. She will always meet my needs. She will always greet me when I get home with a wink, my favorite meal next to my lazy boy, and ESPN on the television. She will always tell me how strong, brilliant, and gifted I am. And she will never nag me."

As the bride and groom are having these thoughts they are paying no attention to me when I say, "Marriage is not to be entered unto unadvisedly, but reverently, discreetly, and in the fear of God." The bride and groom are not really paying attention when I ask them to repeat the words, "for better, for worse, for richer, for poorer, in sickness and in health." Then, sooner or later, one of them disappoints the other by not living up to expectations and real marriage begins. One of them gets sick or one of them becomes difficult to live with and real love and commitment begin. Acceptance, forgiveness, and mutual understanding are born.

Perhaps the couple dreams about having children. They think about little people that look just like them. They think of giggles and bubble gum breath. They think of Christmas, ball games, and ballet classes. They think of their need of being needed. Then children come and they are definitely needed, and the real sacrifice of parenthood is required. They get up in the middle of the night with a crying baby. They lose sleep. Their children develop minds of their own, talk back, and rebel. Their children stay out all night and worry mom and dad sick. Shallow illusions die and real love is born.

All the important things in life cost us. We should not be surprised to find that when the most important person who ever lived spoke about the most important thing we could ever do, he said that sacrifice is required, a cross is required, and death is required. Why? Jesus put it poignantly, "Very truly, I tell you, unless a grain of wheat falls into the earth and dies, it remains just a single grain; but if it dies, it bears much fruit" (John 12:24).

What did Jesus mean by that? What did Jesus mean by all this death business? One of the best illustrations of this for me is seen through an experience of one of my closest friends. His name is Allen Johnson and he is a United Methodist minister. He is also married to a minister. However, there was a time when Allen had other plans for his life. He thought of being a vet. He thought of the kind of woman he would marry, the kind of money he would make, and the kind of life he would lead. None of these thoughts ever included being a pastor or being married to one either!

Allen's life took a different path than he had anticipated. He gave up his plans to be a vet. He gave up his ideas on the money he wanted to make and the lifestyle he would have, and he became a pastor. You would think that would be the end of the story, right? You would think that he made a good decision and was happy and fulfilled, right? Allen felt the cost of his decision one day. He was serving his second appointment as chaplain of Florida Southern College. He was walking around a lake one day and said to himself, "I am in my mid-thirties. I didn't go to vet school. I am not married. I am not making any money. Here I am, a chaplain of this school — a pastor. I am listening to kids complain about life." Then Allen, who is not one to go on about such experiences, said that he felt God speak to him in that moment. Do you know what Allen felt God say to him? After all his complaining about all the things he had given up, Allen said he heard God say, "Allen, now we can get started."

Jesus said, "If a grain of wheat does not fall on the ground and die, it will not bear fruit." Jesus said, "Whoever does not carry the cross and follow me cannot be my disciple."

You see, real life begins when we die to ourselves — when we die to control — when we die to our selfish desires and trivial plans. Real life in Christ begins when we surrender our ego, our pride, and our stubbornness. God can get started on us when we come to the place where we are free from the bondage of trite preoccupations and recognize that our only need is God. This is what it means to die.

There are many who never accept this. This is why there are people who have been Christians all their lives who are never spiritually fulfilled. This is why there are Christians who never grow in their faith. They have never made the decision to be a disciple. Until you become a disciple you will never experience the abundant life. Until you carry a cross and die you can never really live.

If we want God to use us, we must make ourselves available, empty our lives of the things that have become more important than God and allow God to cleanse us and renew us. We must come to the place where we pray, "God, I am tired of doing things on my own. I am tired of thinking I know what is best. I am tired of doing the same things expecting to get different results. I want you to take over my life. I hand all of it over to you. I let go of the things that I have made more important than you and ask you to fill me up. Use me!" If that is your honest prayer, God will move like a tidal wave in your life!

I recall doing a hospital call while I was in seminary that reminded me of the spiritual death that is required of all disciples. I had just started seminary and was visiting patients with a supervisor who was rather unorthodox. He had a way of getting to the truth of things without being abrasive, which is good if you are making your living as a chaplain! We were visiting a patient who was recovering from a drug overdose. The patient was a prominent man in the community. He said to my supervisor, "I have lost everything — my job, my reputation, my livelihood... I have lost it all. This is the end for me." My supervisor responded, "Oh, that's interesting because I see this as just the beginning." The patient responded, "What do you mean, the beginning?" My supervisor said, "Well, you said you have lost everything? Everything?" The patient said, "Yes, everything that really mattered to me." My supervisor replied, "Well, that means God has you all to himself. Just think what he can do with you now."

Come and die. Your life is waiting. Amen.

CPSIA information can be obtained
at www.ICGtesting.com
Printed in the USA
FFOW05n1314080814

9 780788 027871